LIFE'S little LESSONS

100 MICRO ESSAYS

Other Books by Rachel

Essay

Parenthood: Has Anyone Seen My Sanity?
The Life-Changing Madness of Tidying Up After Children
This Life With Boys
Hills I'll Probably Lie Down On
We Count it All Joy
If These Walls Could Talk

Poetry

this is how you know
Life: a definition of terms
The Book of Uncommon Hours
Textbook of an Ordinary Life
this is how you live
sincerely yours: letters in poetry

To see all the books Rachel has written, please click or visit the link below:

www.racheltoalson.com/writing

RACHEL TOALSON

LIFE'S little LESSONS

100 MICRO ESSAYS

BATLEE PRESS

Published by
Batlee Press
Post Office Box 591596
San Antonio, TX 78259

Copyright ©2021 by Rachel Toalson
All rights reserved.
Printed in the United States of America.
Interior design by Toalson Media.
Cover design by Ben Toalson. www.toalsonmarketing.com

No part of this book may be reproduced or transmitted in any form or by any means, electronic or mechanical, including photocopying and recording, or by any information storage and retrieval system, without permission in writing from the publisher. For information regarding permission, write to Batlee Press, PO Box 591596, San Antonio, TX 78259.

The author appreciates your taking the time to read her work. Please consider leaving a review wherever you bought it and telling your friends how much you enjoyed it. Both of those help get the book into the hands of new readers, which is incredibly important for authors. Thank you for your support.
www.racheltoalson.com

Names: Toalson, Rachel, author.
Title: Life's little lessons: 100 micro essays / Rachel Toalson
Description: First edition. | Batlee Press, Texas:
Batlee Press Books, 2021

10 9 8 7 6 5 4 3 2 1

First Edition—2021

To Ben and my sons
When I think about time, I think about you
I love you forever and always

Introduction

As the mom of six sons, it probably goes without saying that I don't often have time to sit down and write a full-fledged essay.

Well, who cares? some might say. Who wants to write an essay, anyway?

The word "essay" tends to invoke a picture, in most minds, of that tedious thing we were all required to write in middle school and high school and probably even college. Five hundred words about how Shakespeare's *Romeo and Juliet* is a metaphor for class issues in the UK. One thousand words on John F. Kennedy's life and presidency in comparison with and contrast to King Arthur's reign in Camelot. Fifteen hundred words on the meaning of the color purple in *The Color Purple*.

These aren't the kinds of essays I'm talking about.

As an adult, I discovered a deep love for the essay form. Little did I know—until I started reading my colleagues, the brilliant greats past and present—that essays could be interesting, playful, poetic, personal. I read a love essay that was really a simplified ode to walking, a comical essay about a man's foray into fashion, a heart-breaking essay about a wife's goodbye to her husband and ultimate coming-to-terms with her own death. The essay could meander, explore, teach, entertain, dream, predict, clarify. It was marvelous.

But when I'm not working on fiction, my writing happens in

short bursts. A poem here, a fragment there, an idea jotted down on this week's grocery list. Long-form essays have long called to me, but the concentration and quiet they require are rarely a part of my life right now. One day I will get to my long list of ideas (or maybe not). But for now, this book full of essays of one hundred, five hundred, maybe the occasional eight hundred words will have to do.

The essays in this book were scribbled down over the course of two or three years. I've tried to arrange them into some sort of thematic order—which means that sometimes, in one section, you will read about a two-year-old youngest child, and in others he will be three, followed by perhaps another where he is barely one. It will be the same with seasons—one essay it's summer, the next fall, the next summer again. The ages and seasons don't matter; I only use them to provide context in the particular story. So bear this information in mind, but don't let it distract you.

And one final note: Personal essays are exactly that—personal. These are my thoughts, dreams, hopes, fears, solutions, wonderings, musings. You may not agree with where I land in any one of them. That's okay—we're different people. But do take what you can, what may be useful to you, and let it blossom in your life.

I hope you are inspired and encouraged by these lessons I've so far gathered in my life.

WONDER

1. Don't Forget Stillness in the Rush of Life

Work, lately, runs away from me.

I've found it difficult to get anything done this summer. I intentionally scaled back a little, said I wanted to spend most of the summer working on research, which has been fun (and addictive...I don't know if I'll ever be done with research).

I've researched pirates, madhouses, carnival architecture, the Industrial Revolution, science, legends and myths, everything about the 1930s, P.T. Barnum, witches, and the expeditions of Captain Cook. These may seem like they have nothing at all to do with each other, but that's the best kind of research a writer can do. The greatest stories come from the intersection between seemingly unconnected ideas and things.

I tagged this summer as a research summer, because I know how hard summers are with all the kids home from school and fighting over every little thing and asking for more food, constantly, and generally existing to tear the house apart.

But when I don't get a chance to write, the words pile up inside me, and I start feeling like a clogged pipe about to burst. The pressure gets immense. I need an outlet.

Not to mention, notes recently came back from my publisher, and I needed time to make the edits. A deadline loomed.

So I started stealing moments where I could. The kids went outside to play for a few minutes, so I opened my journal and started writing, and then one of them would fly back in to tattle on his brother, and I'd find myself annoyed and bent out of shape that he was acting like a kid.

They'd happily play with the LEGOs on the floor, and I'd boot up my computer with the intention of breezing through some edits, and someone would interrupt me with a question, to which I would respond with undisguised frustration—because he was displaying the curiosity of a kid.

They'd sit down to do their silent reading, and I'd pull out a book so I could make a little extra progress on my research, and as soon as I opened the book someone would tap me on the shoulder, smile, and show me a page from his own book, and the look on my face would communicate how exasperated I felt by the interruption.

The other day I cooked dinner while listening to a collection of Hans Christian Andersen's fairy tales, and the back door kept opening so that my sons could come in and tell me about the grasshopper they'd caught and the rabbit they saw and how the birds were eating the bread they left out. I kept feeling that familiar flash of aggravation every time they interrupted—because my hands were messy and I had to push pause on my audiobook. So inconvenient.

And then they all filed back outside and I stood there working in silence, thinking about how I hadn't been able to stop and look at my kids for the entire day. I dropped the dishes I was rinsing and stepped out onto the porch. They were all crowded in the middle of the yard, by a rock they'd lifted, under which lived all sorts of fascinating bugs.

I watched them for a good, long while.

And this is what I noticed:

A little boy's feet streaked with dirt

Long eyelashes splayed against a smooth cheek

A brilliant smile from the one who successfully captured a grasshopper

The studied concentration of a boy trying to poke holes in a plastic container so the caught grasshoppers could breathe

A Batman cape, whipping in the wind

The exuberant laughter of three boys on a trampoline

These words now live in my journal, and I jot some down every day, tiny observations of life.

Our lives brim with inspiration and illumination. They overflow with beauty and magnificence. They contain wonder and LIFE, if we can only stop long enough to see it. It's not easy. I know. There's so much to do, all the time. How will we ever do it all?

I'm not convinced we will. And that's okay. The important thing is that we're living a full life—and the only way we can do that is by stopping, looking, listening, breathing, being.

Standing still.

2. Rise Early to See Wonders

This morning we left before dawn, and as I was walking out the door, something rustled in the rose bushes to my right. The porch lights were on, but shadows blanketed the bushes, and my mind invented all manner of frightening things that might emerge with an intent to eat me—or worse. But it was only a small brown rabbit. I have seen this rabbit, or one very like it, before, hopping around my backyard, chewing on grass. This morning my movement startled it from rose bushes.

Does it live there? Was it merely resting before it slid beneath the slats of my fence? Was it the same rabbit that seems to have taken up residence in our backyard?

I watched its ball of a tail shudder as it hopped away, my mind ticking off wonder.

1. The creatures are up very early this morning.

2. I am up very early this morning.

3. If I had not been up so early this morning, I would have missed this magnificent creature.

4. What other creatures have I missed because I did not get up early?

3. Be Awed By Nature

We stop by a lake to let our sons run, and there's a small metal playground like the ones I used to play on as a child. Everything's turned plastic now, because it's safer; kids won't get as hurt by plastic as they would by metal (I think I still have burn scars from metal slides baking in the sun).

The playground features some metal monkey bars, and my sons head straight for them. But they stop short and shout. My husband and I move to see what all the fuss is about. We bend close. Squint. Tilt our heads. Can we trust our eyes?

All over the metal bars are hundreds of baby asps.

"Don't touch them," my husband warns. "They'll sting you."

But it's impossible not to draw closer, stare at the tiny pieces of nature inching from white sacs. They slide from shells, glide along the bars, float on strings to who knows where.

So many of them that the bars look alive. My youngest son squeezes my arm. I don't want him to be afraid, so I take him a little closer. "Don't touch them," I repeat. "Just look at them."

I look at my sons, all their eyes fastened on these tiny fascinating creatures—keeping a safe distance but observing nonetheless. Some of their mouths drop open in awe. Some of them wear expressions of mild fear.

I smile.

And think.

And consider that fear mixed with awe is an appropriate

response to nature. They know these asps can hurt them, but, at the same time, they are mesmerized by them. We stand there for half an hour, watching the baby asps inch along the bars and do what my sons wish they could do—cross the monkey bars.

My head swarms with nature's fears and fascinations—spiders, tornadoes, snakes, bees. So many wonders. So many mysteries. So many dangers.

Perhaps this is true of all nature—it is by turns fascinating and frightening, an unknown sort of world that can, at best, only be observed—from a safe distance.

4. Pay Attention to the Feet

I stood in line, waiting to vote. I hadn't planned on a line so long in the middle of the day, but I had just finished a doctor's appointment. So fortunately I had a book with me.

Lines don't matter so much when you have a book.

When reading in public, I never feel completely immersed the way I'd like to be; people are generally interesting, and my gaze wanders to them often. So when a side door in the hallway where I waited with others opened, I didn't find it unusual that my attention was split by the man at the door.

He rested his weight on a metal walker, the kind with black ends, not the kind with tennis balls stabilizing it. His eyes roved over all of us in line, and he opened his mouth as though to speak, but no words came out. The woman behind him—his daughter? a caretaker? a family friend?—rested one hand on his back while she held open the door with the other.

He shuffled halfway through the door, then halted. His face took on a serious concentration it hadn't held before. His feet, instead of continuing their onward walk, danced in place, a quick-stepped shuffle. I watched them, fascinated.

A convulsion of accident or one of excitement? Perhaps a little of both.

When his feet finished their dancing, the man continued on his way, at what would be an agonizing pace for me but one that was likely just fine for him. In the five feet between the door leading outside and the door opening into the voting room, he danced twice more, each one no less astonishing than the last.

Later that day, my orange tabby cat, named River Dash Toalson by my sons for his paradoxical soothing personality and ferocious play, paused at his water container. As he bent to drink, his front paws danced as though he were trying to unearth something. The dance reminded me of the old man I had watched, who did his civic duty and voted, dancing all the way.

In the moments of our most routine action, perhaps it is the feet that tell the truest story.

5. Let Nature's Resilience Show You Yourself

The sun lent a golden light to the sidewalks as we wound our way through the city zoo. The day was crisp, cold at the edges, and perfect for a day of visiting animals.

I always feel a little conflicted when it comes to watching animals at the zoo, because on the one hand it is sad to see them changed in captivity and on the other it is fascinating to view them up close from a safe, contained distance. To watch the mesmerizing way they move, to stare into their strange eyes, to communicate beyond the language barrier.

My sons headed straight for the bears and then to the monkeys, where they watched the little ones pick and play. I watched a mother whose baby monkey walked all over her face and clung to her back and bit her tail while she did not flinch through any of it, and I marveled at her patience. I feel the intrusion of my young every day, and I am not nearly so forgiving.

We stopped for a while to observe some ducks and an exhibit of turtles, but my eye was drawn to a black swan with a plume of feathers rising from its back, looking like a wealthy southern belle in a ballgown. Feathers glistened in the wind, one turning circles in the water, caught in her wake. She ventured near us. Her exhibit included a fifty-cent machine where you could purchase pellets of food, but I did not have change, and she moved away. I was struck by her beauty and regal majesty. A queen among birds is what her grace and glamor seemed to say.

While my sons disappeared into a bird house and I stayed out with my youngest son, still in a stroller that couldn't be rolled into the house, I peered into a massive open cage where larger birds strutted. A white secretary bird paced as though agitated, and in five noisy beats of his wings, he thrust himself against the top of the enclosure, a net that looked like the kind trapeze artists use when training. The net stretched around his body, folded around his wings, and flung him back toward the ground. He let loose the kind of sound that made heads turn, the kind that made my heart turn in recognition.

I have felt that captivity before.

The natural world seems far removed from us and yet it has the ability to mirror ourselves back to us in unexpected ways. We can measure ourselves by the patience of a mother monkey, the elegance of a black swan, the momentary blinding rage that besets a secretary bird before he calms to pace between his fenceposts, content to make whatever he can of another day.

6. Look for the Everyday Magic in the World

The world is breathtaking.

The other day, as my family and I drove to church, the clouds looked as though they were a rolling white-and-gray ocean, a collection of froth and waves, a layered landscape that begged for attention. My husband was driving, so I snapped pictures, which, of course, did not do the beauty justice. I am no Oliver Pike or Andreas Feininger, though I am a great admirer of nature photography.

I pointed out the spectacle to my children, who paused their backseat arguing to express their awe (they are as enamored with the natural world as their mother).

"It looks like an ocean," one of them said.

"It looks like we're driving under the ocean," another of them said.

"It looks like…" A third could think of nothing to add.

"Like we're driving upside down, under a sea of gray waves," I said.

They all laughed at the image—driving upside down!—and agreed.

The clouds, that day, looked like magic. (The interior of our car also felt like magic; my sons did not resume their argument after my interruption. Maybe the clouds really *were* magical.)

I believe that everyday magic (one might call it miracles) exists everywhere—we just have to know how to look for it. We simply have to open our eyes, fasten them on a point, let the wonder steal into our bones and take us where we have not been before.

I see magic when one of my sons brings me a flower

I smell magic when my oven is baking homemade brownies

I feel magic when my husband gives me a head massage after a headache-y kind of day

I taste magic when chocolate melts in my mouth

I hear magic in music—symphonies or top radio hits, it doesn't matter

The world doesn't always seem like the most interesting thing; we can spend days and weeks and months feeling like we always see or hear or taste or feel or smell the same old things. We have to intentionally look to notice this everyday magic, which does not announce itself but often flutters in on a whisper. (Or maybe we need to make more brownies—who can say?)

We see everyday magic when people are kind to each other, when a story is read to a child, when love wins (love is always a magical thing).

All it takes to witness everyday magic is to see it—to say, "Ah, look. There it is."

There it is. Do you see it?

7. Let Yourself Be Enamored By the Small Things

This evening, on the drive home from church, I found myself so enamored with the pattern of golden sunlight and shadow on the tops of the trees that the world inside our minivan faded away.

We make this drive every week, but today was the longest day of the year, and we left a little later, caught by conversations and community. The sun, to our delight, was still happy to smile and bathe the land in a glossy glow. Halfway through the trip back my husband asked me what I was doing, why I was so quiet, why I stared so intently out the window. I told him I was trying to figure out why certain trees were lit by the sun and others stood in darkness. The pattern didn't seem to have much of a pattern at all—or make any kind of scientific sense, for that matter.

We agreed that while it looked random on the ground, it probably made perfect sense in the sky.

It made me wish I were a pilot, if for only a second.

8. Embrace Imaginative Falsehoods

When I was a kid, I had a grand imagination. I would imagine all sorts of things—monsters chasing me down a hallway, hungry oversized wolves waiting right outside my window, dark figures illuminated by the lightning storm.

Even better (or worse, however you want to look at it) I had a dark imagination. Still do. My husband made me watch the first season of *Stranger Things*—which was amazing, by the way—and I can't be in a room alone anymore.

But often, when I exercised my imagination or I created an elaborate fantasy in my mind, I would always feel a little guilty. This was because, as a kid, I was told over and over and over again not to lie. Fantasy—the things that I created in my mind—felt like lies. A dragon wasn't real. A person could never fly. I did not own a pair of the fastest boots in the world.

A couple of years ago, my husband and I were having a bit of trouble with our second son, who felt the need to lie when we noticed he'd gotten into food—especially sugary food. Treats were his weakness (aren't they everyone's?), and if any were left in a kid-reachable area, he found them. Maybe they called to him, like they do to me.

When asked about it, my son would tell an elaborate story. And my husband and I would talk to him about the importance of telling the truth—how when one doesn't tell the truth, one runs the risk of others not trusting him anymore—and trust is of utmost importance.

And all of that is true.

Lying, to tell the truth, ignites my anger. I can't stand being lied to. It's one of the most offensive offenses. When my children are sneaking around or lying to me about things, I often lecture them far more than is necessary. They get the point.

But then my husband and I watched a TED talk about how lying sometimes indicates that children are extremely creative and ingenious, because they create elaborate stories in order to get out of trouble. The speaker said that rather than condemning that attribute, a parent should, if not encourage it exactly, at least celebrate it. Something as simple as, "Well, that's a really creative story, son, but we know you got into the chocolate chip cookies, and we expect you to tell the truth in our house. You can write your creative story on paper instead."

It's a subtle shift: this statement that says imagining a creative story is an acceptable thing—when recorded on a bit of paper and not used to tell a lie.

I think often about this dichotomy. When I first started writing fiction, the story I told was my mother's story. I could not reach inside myself and tell the false stories that I had to tell, because they felt wrong. I didn't want to lie. I had been scolded as a child for lying—just like I had scolded my own children. It took me a while to get past that reluctance to lie and to see this kind of lying—using the imagination to create something from nothing—as a good and beautiful thing.

But now that I have, my characters have become real people. It seems strange—even a little disturbing sometimes. Every character I write about takes a place in my life, and they remain with me forever. Whether I'm writing a kid's book, an adult novel, or poetry that may not be the least bit true (because you never know when metaphor comes to play), my characters become real and breathing people who change my life as much as I change theirs.

Our language around lying has changed. While it is still a known expectation that our sons will always tell us the truth, often what we'll say after they get in trouble for doing something wrong is "Now go tell a story that would absolve you of your crime."

Because this is cultivating imagination and creativity.

9. Enjoy the Wonder of Nature

It's colder than I expected it to be, for April.

The wind whispers through the trees, twirling leaves, flattening some, rippling others. Birds dart through the sky, as though the wind has energized them. They call out to each other, playing chase or tag or some marriage of the two.

The sky is sharp blue, wisps of clouds pulled through it like bits of cottony, willowy thread. The trees hiss, my sons shriek, someone in the distance works on a roof. I breathe in the smell of grass, moist dirt, the unmistakable cool of peppermint, rising from my tea.

Here I am, witnessing.

It is impossible to sit out in this beauty without setting it to memory, without recording green, brown, blue, white, shadow, light, life.

It brims with life.

And we are the same—human and nature—for a moment in time.

Then the air gusts, whips my hair against my cheek. It stings and soothes, in equal measure, reminding me that today I am alive.

Today I am alive.

And today I will live.

10. Own Your Wrong Answer

The littlest one, still a baby with emerging speech, splashes in my bath tub, playing with some cars his older brothers left there. He keeps holding them up, guessing their colors, most of which he gets wrong. He laughs every time he states "red" and the car's color is, in actuality, orange. He eyes me with a mischievous smile, and I am struck by how unselfconscious he is about his inaccurate guesses. He corrects himself and immediately holds up another and attempts another guess.

We are born, it seems, knowing that being wrong doesn't change who we are.

When do we lose this comfort with the wrong answer, this positive relationship with correction? And what are we missing once we do?

11. Creatures Speak if We Listen

The birds are singing just outside my window, some of them insistent, like they have something important to say, some of them relaxed in a way that speaks of family and maybe new chicks living in their nests among the rafters of my house. I watch how they dart about, a black blot in the morning sky. The chatter breaks the silence of sleep.

I am alone for now. It's always good to be alone and yet know and understand that you are not alone, not really, because something beautiful awaits you just outside your window.

Here is the melody of their song:

1. It is a beautiful day to be alive.
2. I am here.
3. Hear me sing.

They are singing a song I don't understand, but it is a song I know.

12. Never Accept Shame for Your Body's Amazing Abilities

I picked up my bass guitar, swung it over my shoulder, and felt the horrifying rush every woman has felt at some point in her life.

I remember girls in junior high and high school calling parents for an extra pair of pants, their faces red and blotchy as they sat in the nurse's office, waiting. It never happened to me, fortunately, but we were all ill-equipped to handle the betrayal of our bodies then; every month we were still as surprised as we ever were to walk into the bathroom, see the rose bloom on our panties, and feel the shame burning our cheeks as we walked back out to admit, in low, hopefully-not-overheard voices that we hadn't brought the necessary supplies to school with us that morning.

Turns out not much changes over the years, except you know what's happened without even visiting the bathroom.

I felt the panic blossom like the blood was doing, invisibly for now (but for how long?). I put my guitar down, mumbled something incoherent to my husband, and scurried away.

Safely closed and locked away in the bathroom, it was just as bad as I'd imagined. The blood had stained my underwear and made a nice red look-at-me dot on the back of my jeans—an almost perfect circle.

Thankfully, I had brought supplies with me (you learn some things in the twenty-three years between First Period and Billionth Period). I cleaned up as best I could; there wasn't much to be done about the perfect round spot on my jeans. I scrubbed frantically, like an embarrassed twelve-year-old, but I only succeeded in smearing the rust color more.

I sat in that bathroom for a few minutes, gulping down my shame, trying to think through possible solutions—I could claim a headache and sit in the back of the church; I could tell my husband I'd been hit by a case of Severe Diarrhea (tell me: Why is that less embarrassing than admitting I'd leaked blood because of my period? Ironic.); I could hide away in the car where no one could find me. I didn't like any of the options. Maybe subconsciously I knew I couldn't let a period keep me from singing.

Still, my cheeks burned as I opened the bathroom door. I stood through the whole music set, worried that the piano player, positioned behind me, would find his eyes drawn to my backside and see the spot and know…what, exactly? That I'm a woman? That I bleed?

Why are we so ashamed of this natural cycle of womanhood? Why do I feel my cheeks, still, flaming as I write this, as I think about people *reading* it? Why are women made to feel like this thing they cannot control, this cycle of blood and eggs and potential new life, is an altogether disgusting one? Women used to paint on caves with their menstrual blood.

I want to be that kind of woman. Not…literally, but, you know, figuratively. Brave. Unashamed. Proud, even.

Can I be proud to bleed?

Menstruation makes others (particularly males)

uncomfortable. Women used to be banished outside the camp of their community until the flow of their blood ceased (though, honestly, sometimes I'd like to live outside the camp, if only for a moment of peace from all the males in my house). They were declared "unclean."

We're still made to feel like we're unclean.

But without this natural cycle of womanhood life would not continue.

So next time my body's natural cycle comes to visit unexpectedly, with one perfectly placed dot, maybe I'll wear it like a badge, instead of hiding away in a church bathroom, scrubbing away the evidence that I am a woman.

Maybe I'll be brave. Unashamed.

Proud.

13. Listen to the Wisdom of the Natural World

On the way to an event my husband was filming, a Tough Mudder where a woman with cerebral palsy was competing, we drove past an area of Texas that, a few years ago, was almost completely destroyed by dangerous brush fires. The fires decimated most of the woods in that area, and as I looked at those stark, leafless trees, the ones still standing, among the pocket of green ones with their leaves budding for summer, I could not tear my eyes from the broken ones. They were still trying, still lifting their limbs to the sky, their branches like crooked fingers reaching for something they might never get again—life.

But still reaching. Still…hoping. In a way.

The sky was a perfect blue, and the green contrast of the living trees proved life still existed in that area. But those trees. Those broken trees, crooked and knotted. They had not been felled by the fire but remained upright, even while many around them collapsed. They were gray, not black, like you would expect from burned-up trees. Whoever had cleared the forests of charred trunks and limbs had left those particular skinny, seemingly lifeless sticks. They had seen some sign of life in those bent trees, something that indicated maybe they would live in spite of the inferno. Maybe they would bud again. Maybe they would add another ring to their life.

I wondered, then, how many in our world are like those

trees, appearing, at first glance, to have nothing to offer the world; walking around gray and knotted; still reaching their fingers up toward the thing they need most—light, hope, life.

How like them am I, in my broken places? Do I keep standing when others fall? Do I carry on in spite of the inferno?

Do I see light? Do I feel hope? Do I reach for life?

LOVE

14. Don't Take Unkindness So Personally

I was stirring some oatmeal, having already ruined a pot with cayenne pepper when I mistakenly grabbed it instead of the cinnamon. I was still recovering from a particularly horrid flu, and my brain wasn't exactly in prime health.

And because my usually competent brain felt foggy and unfocused (or, perhaps, in spite of it...though my life often feels like a tapestry of irony), my second son chose this morning to ask me, "What makes people be mean to each other?"

I flicked down the burner, knowing that this question would take all of my attention to answer. I stirred one more time before turning around to face him. I said, "What makes you be unkind to your brothers?"

He shrugged.

"Sometimes when you feel angry, are you unkind?" I said.

His eyebrows went up. "Oh. Yeah."

"Or if you feel sad, sometimes you say something unkind, right?" I said.

"I think I understand," he said. I could see that he was thinking, turning over my words in his mind. I wanted to add another important thought.

"People aren't usually unkind without some reason. They feel sad, they feel angry, they feel disappointed, they feel lonely. Those feelings are hard for them to feel. They're hard for any of us to feel." I looked at him to see if he was still listening. You don't have much more than a few seconds with kids. But his blue eyes fastened on me, like he waited for more. By this time, his brothers had joined him at the table, and they were all listening.

"Sometimes people choose unkindness because they think it will make them feel better. It never does," I said.

My son shook his head.

"We should always work to figure out why people are being unkind," I said.

We've been telling him and all his brothers this very thing since they were all too young to understand it. In fact, it's hidden in many of our family values: believe the best about people and seek to find out why they make the choices they make. Don't judge. Accept, embrace, and help heal their hurts.

Be gentle.

Love the unlovable. Find the lonely and make them feel full. Defend the defenseless.

They can hear the shift in our voices when we talk about these things—the slight hitch in our breath, the upward turn of our tone, the urgency of words and sound that fly straight from our hearts. They know it's important—no, vital—to listen.

When I turned back to stir the oatmeal, it had burned a little on the bottom.

But no one complained.

15. Love In Spite of Fear

The fear flamed up fast. There I was reading in a research book, and I happened to notice I had missed a call on my phone. I had a new message. The number was vaguely familiar, so I paused my work, which I never do, and listened to the message. It was the dermatologist's office. My doctor had removed a mole six days ago, a wonky red one that I thought, like the others that have been removed periodically over the years, was harmless.

Severely atypical, the woman on the phone said. She was not my doctor. She did not need to be. The warm rush of panic welled, and I listened to the rest of her instructions—make another appointment, take more skin, complete a biopsy—from a very long distance away. She finished her message by saying my doctor would talk to me about what happened from here.

What would happen from here?

My husband was out with his brother, who was visiting from North Carolina. I didn't want to disturb him with the news.

I texted my mom instead. She is twenty-six years older than I am. We exchanged messages. I felt better.

But my mood plummeted. I fell into a dark hole of imagining what life would be like without my mother, how I would find peace in the absence of her, "It will be okay. You'll see."

Life is a difficult pendulum to navigate, black-edged despair darkening a golden day, an inexplicable light clinging to the night.

I don't know if I'll ever understand it, how fear can be so tangled up in love.

Maybe, though, it's enough to know you can't have one without the other.

And love anyway.

16. Motherly Moments Deserve Extra Attention

He languished by the lamp, head drooping, book in his hand. I sat beside him. "You feeling okay?" I said. I already knew the answer, but I asked it anyway.

He didn't even speak; he only shook his head. I could feel the heat radiating from his skin; he had all the outward signs of the flu.

I took him in my arms, let him rest his head against me. The possibility of contagion doesn't bother a mama whose son is battling sickness. So though I was the only one in my house who hadn't gotten a flu shot this year, I rocked my son because he needed me.

I read stories. I rubbed essential oils on his chest. I let him sleep in my arms—because he is getting bigger and he will not always let me—or need me—to do this. I held him as long as I could, as long as he needed.

And though I am glad my son does not suffer from sickness often, or sickness that is terminal, I enjoyed the time I had with a four-year-old who didn't feel like bouncing out of my arms before I was ready.

I soaked up the sleepy moments, which lasted only two days.

Today he is racing in and out of rooms, flinging flowers at me, trying to find where he put his shoes so he can go out back and sword fight with sticks.

The smell of him clings to my shirt.

17. Gratitude May Not Cure Burnout, But it Helps

Lately I've been feeling burned out. It's a carryover from the end of the year, sliding into the new year, though I took two weeks off work to read and spend time with my kids and relax.

It's not the work that has me so burned out; in fact, work, right now, feels like a necessary respite from the domestic world. It's everything else—the lunches that need making, the house that needs tidying, the kids who need constant supervision.

I told my husband the other day that I almost feel like I can't let our sons out of my sight, even though the oldest three are twelve, nine, and eight—ages at which I was already staying home alone, for extended periods of time. But today's parents live in a culture of fear—fear of what will happen to our kids if we take our eyes off them and fear of what will happen to us if other people see that we've taken our eyes off our kids. We've all heard the horror stories—parents (usually mothers) arrested for leaving their kid in the car for five minutes while they run into the store for some toilet paper or for letting their kid walk to or play in the park alone or for leaving them home alone while they run to the grocery store for an hour of blissful no-kids shopping. We are afraid, and so we protect from real (the repercussions of concerned citizens reporting on our perceived neglect) and imagined (child abduction, which is a percentage so low it would require leaving your kid alone for 750,000 years, according to some experts) dangers. At all hours. Every day. At a significant cost to ourselves.

Because of this, our kids don't know how to be alone or how to care for themselves. My twelve-year-old didn't even know how to make a pot of tea, and when, one day, he woke up feeling a little stuffy in the sinuses, he asked me to make him some. This wouldn't otherwise be a problem; most days I'd be happy to make my stuffy-nosed son some echinacea tea, but this particular day I was busy getting breakfast on the table for his five brothers. So I told him to do it himself. He said, "But I don't know how."

Our kids, understandably, have trouble taking care of themselves in our overprotected world, so it's no surprise that my most frequent burnout is parenting burnout. Mothering burnout. I feel exhausted often with what is required of me— keeping my sons out of trouble, monitoring technology time, encouraging creativity, teaching them to clean up after themselves. Making sure I don't become a target for "concerned citizens" calling Child Protective Services.

The burnout isn't completely caused by the protective requirement, of course. I do, after all, have six sons, and that means there are lots of needs around my house. But the break I might occasionally get from leaving my kids alone to go for a walk certainly contributes to my exhaustion.

So it was with this persistent and pervasive burnout that I began this new year by picking up the book, *Wave*, by Sonali Deraniyagala.

In this book, Deraniyagala loses her two sons—her husband and parents, too—in a tsunami while on vacation. The same things that, upon waking up, pull down that cloud of annoyance —shoes left in the middle of the floor, drawings littering the furniture in never-ending piles of paper, pleas for breakfast and complaints once it's delivered—were things she would never experience again. She would not watch her sons navigate the explosive time of puberty, would not ever remind them to do their homework, would not break up another argument about something ridiculous.

When I finished the book, on a five-mile run on the treadmill in my garage, which doubles as my sons' LEGO playroom, I stood there for a minute, my heart rate slowing, my breath evening, my eyes caught on the mess. What would I miss about my sons if the unthinkable happened?

Everything.

I moved back into the kitchen, where my sons sat sipping smoothies, the noise at the table almost at an intolerable level. I kissed them each in turn as they swatted me away ("You're so sweaty, Mama!") and smiled to myself, words thrumming through my head: *I'm so glad they're here.*

Even the shoe I tripped over on my way upstairs couldn't dampen the force of my gratitude and love.

A moment, seized with both hands.

18. Parenthood is for Better or Worse

It's when you think you're done with the meltdowns, the violent flinging of anything within reach, the loud and indignant protestations, the yelling, the angry words, the head pounding, the uncontrollable flailing, the murmured words, the attempts at regulation, the sudden flashes of temper like fireworks exploding in a face, the slamming, the destroying, the long and seemingly endless episodes, the interminable wails, the great and immeasurable grief, the shaking sobs, the regret, the commandeered time.

It's when you think you're done with the meltdowns, because surely he's grown out of them, that they broadside you again, that you take a deep and cleansing breath, that you remember, ah, yes, this is what it feels like to love a child unconditionally.

19. Don't Forget that We Belong to Each Other

It's a brutal world out there.

The climate of our country, currently, is a wild, fierce, fiery summer of seemingly eternal proportions. We are burning ourselves, we are burning each other, we are burning the opinions and viewpoints that do not align with our own. The smoke stings our eyes, blisters our throats, constricts our breath. We ball up and try to survive in our corners. We talk and talk and talk and forget that one of the most important things we can do is simply listen.

And in this place of me against you, us against them, human against human, we all lose.

For most of my life, I have been obsessed with stories. Not just the stories I can create while I'm tucked away in my room for a few hours every day or the magnificent stories I can read in the pages of a book. I'm talking about the stories of others.

I have listened to stories with rapt attention as I sat across the room from an interviewee and jotted down notes in a reporter's notebook. I have listened to stories with nothing in my hands, only a watchful eye and invested heart. And I have listened to stories with a mind reeling to grasp the words I want to say before I've even fully heard the person with whom I'm engaged, more intent on my own story than another's.

So, you see, I have work to do.

Recently I invited into my home a young teenage girl who

has attempted, multiple times, to commit suicide. These attempts were demanded by a dark depression that would not let her go. I listened to her story of loneliness, acute pain, misunderstanding, trauma, misery. Later, after she'd left, I paged through the journals she'd left me with a clipped "I don't want them anymore. I was going to burn them." I cried, I raged, I ached for the girl who'd felt so alone and burdensome in her despair that suicide was the only logical conclusion. I held her heart in my hands, gently, willingly. Hopefully. We were connected by our shared humanity. And when I finished reading, I understood teenage suicide better.

This is what happens when we sit face to face with someone who is different from us and we listen to their story.

My husband, Ben, engaged in a long and random conversation with a homeless woman out on the streets of Austin, Texas, where he and I were attending a business conference. I didn't join him immediately, because their conversation was so animated that I assumed she was one of the other conference attendees, rather than a woman who lived on the streets. I was engaged in my own conversation. But then he bought her lunch and introduced her to me. She gratefully took the food he offered, hugged him, and called him an angel. She is a light to the homeless, she said, because she keeps them on the straight and narrow. And who are we to argue with a purpose like that? Perhaps it is only our place to listen to a broken woman with most of her teeth missing. And when we finish listening, we understand the homeless a little better.

This is what happens when we stand face to face with someone who is different from us and we listen to their story.

When I scroll through social media feeds (though, to

confess, I don't do it often anymore, because it's too painful) and see the ways we are so glued to our corners that we come out fighting with the least little provocation, when I see how much we assume about people who are different than we are, when I consider the fear that keeps us safe and curled up in our protective shells and insulated opinions rather than boldly listening to the stories of real people, I can clearly see how we have shifted into such a combative place.

We've traded individual people for representative groups, and our opinions and assumptions paint them with broad, general strokes. Lazy. Lying. Selfish. Despicable. Making much ado about nothing.

It's easier to dehumanize people when we assign them to groups. It's not as easy when we look in the individual's eyes.

The stories of others can teach us important things: what it means to grow up Black in America, what it means to be poor in America, what it's like being a woman in science or technology or any other field in which pay gaps exist, who the homeless really are, why people attempt or commit suicide, why addiction is so hard to overcome. Regardless of what we think and believe about any of these issues, the best thing we can do to better understand them is to consider that perhaps we don't know everything there is to know and then listen to the people who have lived lives marked by them.

Alfred, Lord Tennyson once said, "I am a part of all that I have met," and if these word are true, if we are, in fact, part of all we meet, then it's also true that we belong to each other. And if we belong to each other, that means there is no me against you, us against them, human against human.

When my oldest son was younger and had periodic

meltdowns during which his legs and arms flailed wildly and he shouted things he didn't really mean, the best way to calm him down was to wrap our arms around him and whisper, "This is hard. I am here. You are safe."

Our world is reeling. We are completely polarized from each other, suspicious, defensive, ready for a fight. Who will be the first to cross the bridge, approach the other side, wrap arms around a perceived enemy and whisper, "This is hard. I am here. You are safe. Tell me your story, because I'm ready to listen."?

20. Try Also to Belong to Yourself

I have a quote attached to my cork board right above my desk, and it reads:

"My wish for you is that you continue. Continue to be who you are, to astonish a mean world with your acts of kindness."

—Maya Angelou

During my writing sessions, I often find my eyes wandering to this quote. It reminds me to write my truth. When I read an unfavorable review, this quote reminds me to keep on creating. When I receive an ugly email or a vicious note, this quote reminds me to continue being exactly who I am. When I feel alone, this quote bolsters me in my wilderness.

I had the privilege of hearing Maya Angelou speak when I was in college. In fact, I had the privilege of covering her speech for the student newspaper, which means I got to shake her hand and look in her eyes and be changed by this brief meeting. It was one of my favorite moments in life, because Angelou has always been a hero of mine. I'm sure she didn't remember a nineteen-year-old girl after leaving the Texas State University campus, but I will remember that meeting for the rest of my life.

She was a pillar of beauty, strength, grace, forgiveness. She exuded love by her very being.

To be like her. To be courageous enough to be who I am, to astonish a mean world with acts of kindness. To simply continue.

How will we do this?

Bill Moyers, an American journalist, once asked Angelou some vital questions:

Moyers: Do you belong anywhere?
Angelou: I haven't yet.
Moyers: Do you belong to anyone?
Angelou: More and more. I mean, I belong to myself. I'm very proud of that. I am very concerned about how I look at Maya. I like Maya very much. I like the humor and courage very much. And when I find myself acting in a way that isn't...that doesn't please me—then I have to deal with that.

This is it. This is what I saw as an inexperienced nineteen-year-old, meeting Maya Angelou for the first time. This is what I saw all over her written works, which I have read and re-read over the course of my life. She belonged to herself. The whole world could come against her—and, in fact, it tried many times—and she would still stand on her feet and say, "I am still here, continuing."

Every day, when I drop off my sons at their school, I hug them tightly and say, "I love you. Have a wonderful day. Remember who you are: strong, kind, courageous, and mostly my son." This is their mission: to continue being who they are.

Some things in this world don't make the least bit of sense. People rail against the choices we make in our lives. Criticism knocks our knees out from under us. Circumstances beat us down. Life is hard. In a perfect life, cancer doesn't come out of the blue and steal the seemingly endless future of someone you love. Hate mail doesn't sail through the cyber waves. There is no violence.

But this is not a perfect world. Sometimes it is incredibly

difficult to continue—continue loving, continue spreading kindness, continue being who we are.

But my wish, like Angelou's, is for you to continue. Continue to be who you are, to shock—no, astonish—the world with your acts of kindness and mercy and grace. With your love.

21. Always Be Love

My love month is October.

This is the month when I celebrate walking down the aisle in an old historical church situated inside a lovely wood near a lake, at the end of which was the man I loved. The evening of October 11, 2003, was the night when my husband and I looked at one another and promised forever—promised, essentially, that we would break the generations of divorce that marked our family lines. It was the night we walked down an enchanted path lined with deer (just like the princesses had in the fairy tales I'd loved as a child). It was the night we held hands across a stick shift, on our way to a magical Disney World honeymoon.

This year we celebrate fifteen years married.

We try, every year, to remind our sons about the birthday of our marriage. We tell stories of falling in love, laughing with our sons about the miscommunication mishaps, bungled dates, and the fumbling of our feet along the path to forever. Sometimes we take out the old albums and relive the days when we were young and practically carefree, basking in the memories of a time we can hardly recall. Sometimes we dance in our kitchen while our sons do chores around us and pretend to gag at our show of affection.

For the last several weeks, I've been wrestling, as I always seem to do, with this idea of love. I have always been a person given to romance—but romantic love is not the only love I think about. In fact, most of the time the kind of love I think about is the one that extends to all humanity—the one that connects us to each other. The one that often feels difficult to choose. The one that does not always come easily or naturally.

My second son asked me the other day why some people are so difficult to love. He had been bickering all day with his next-in-line brother, who is only fourteen months younger than he is. They currently wear the same size clothes—yet another opportunity for contention in their relationship: whose shirt is whose?

I did not answer his question, because there was a larger question on the table, a larger teaching to be made. A teaching about the nature of love—one so important I could not let it go.

When we are in the presence of someone we consider difficult (which is, of course, always subjective), love can feel nearly impossible. But love is not always something that wells up in us and overflows onto all those around us; it is, most frequently, something we must purposefully put on.

We put on our love. We gird ourselves with love. We clothe ourselves with love, arm ourselves with love, fortify ourselves with love. We focus our eyes on love. We train ourselves to become love.

When we move out into the world—into our schools, our neighborhoods, our workplaces, our social media spaces—we must first put on our love. When we engage in conversation (particularly the heated ones), we must put on our love. When we move about in our homes, we must put on our love.

When our emotions overwhelm us, we must stop, breathe, and reach for love—so that we can put it on.

Love is how we see each other clearly. It is how we learn

from one another. It is how we grow ourselves.

Mary Renault famously said: "In hatred as in love, we grow like the thing we brood upon. What we loathe, we graft into our very soul."

What we love—who we love—we graft into our very soul. The more we think about, embrace, put on love, the more we become it.

I hope we can always be love.

RELATIONSHIPS

22. Read Together Always

My ten-year-old son told me last night that he thinks he's done with baths. Baths where he soaked while I read him stories. For the last ten years.

I knew it was coming—he is, after all, ten—but you're never ready, are you? It's so hard to watch children grow up.

Over the years we've read Judy Blume, Rudyard Kipling, R.L. Stine, Robert Louis Stevenson, Mary Downing Hahn, J.K. Rowling, Charles Dickens, Jonathan Stroud, Jonathan Auxier, L.M. Montgomery, Laura Ingalls Wilder, E.B. White, Jacqueline Woodson, Jason Reynolds, and so many more. We've read about space flight, aliens, the intricacies of caves, the world's newest inventions, the Civil Rights movement, desegregation, foreign cultures, natural life, environmentalism and preservation, and so much more.

The discussions we've had over these books and periodicals and stories, the moments we laughed or got choked up (usually me) or learned something entirely new, the ways we were shaped, together, by what we read, together, are forevermore imprinted on who we are.

We will never lose that. Neither will we lose the memories associated with what we've read, even if that sacred reading time has now passed. Digested words, like memories, live in us forever.

My son will still join his brothers for a read-aloud time in our house. Our family gathers around a story every evening. But his bath time, when it was just him and me, has become shower time. He has become an adolescent. I have become an outsider of sorts.

But we will always have the last ten years of bonding over stories.

Pick up a book. Read to your child. You'll never be sorry for the small moment in time when you put down your phone or your to-do list or all those dirty dishes and forged unbreakable bonds around a story.

23. Don't Forget to Call Your Sister

My sons act silly at the table tonight. I watch them in silence for a while, talking to each other, laughing, saying coded things I can't hope to decode. They smile, wiggle, make their own signs, play the Try Not to Laugh game, and I have a sudden glimpse of who they'll be as teenagers. The light snags on my oldest son's face, and he grins at his brother and leans forward and smacks him on the shoulder, a playful punch. The table erupts in loud merriment, and I find it hard not to smile myself.

There is something sacred and beautiful about brotherly love.

Tonight, I call my sister.

24. Let Kindness Connect You to Others

Today I had a routine appointment with my doctor, to check blood work and weight and all the normal yearly box-checking things. I settled into a main lobby chair to wait, hoping the wait wouldn't be long.

A bent man shuffled in with a walker, asked the receptionist for something, then shuffled back toward the front door. I knew he would need help with that door—not only was it heavy, but he had a white package tucked under one arm and both hands gripped the silver bars of his walker. So I jumped from my seat and held the door for him. He said, "Thank you, ma'am," and I practically burst with the joy of one moment of kindness, one moment of helpfulness.

It was a small thing, but there is such great pleasure in helping someone else, without regard for what he looks like or how she smells or how much or little help they need.

The old man sitting two seats down from me in the waiting room said, "I know what that's like. I had back surgery recently, and I could hardly get any doors open."

We engaged in a short conversation after I asked him why he'd had surgery—something I thought I'd never do, considering he was a stranger, but my curiosity won the day—and by the time the nurse called me back, I felt so connected to my fellow humans that I was not even the slightest bit annoyed by the hour I spent waiting for my doctor in a too-cold room.

25. Remember You are Capable of More Than You Think

It's Mother's Day today.

Tomorrow my husband will take his first out-of-state trip away since we've been married. Fourteen years of having him by my side. The next three days he'll work a job we need him to work, but that doesn't make the separation any less difficult.

I've spent the day trying not to think about his departure, trying to think positively, trying to believe that I will be okay.

Will I be okay?

It is, after all, me, a woman, against six young boys. Not against; it's too early to suggest I will be against them. But it will be me, a solo parent, caring for six boys.

My throat feels tight with panic. My mind has already run through all the things that could possibly go wrong, all the difficulties I might meet during transitions and discipline moments, all the pleasures I will not be able to enjoy during work or personal time.

I will miss him. I will miss his body next to mine, the way he breathes in his sleep, his good morning every morning. I will miss his smile, his kiss, his arms at the end of a long day.

He's packing. I'm writing. Tomorrow I will wake him up at the same time I wake our children for their walk to school. And I will count down the hours until he is back home with me, where he belongs.

This is the first time I will have ever been alone in one state, with six children, while he's in another. I admire single parents, but I have never wanted to be one.

But I will parent through the panic.

Why am I panicked? I have asked myself this question so many times, and it is not an answer that comes readily. Perhaps I don't like feeling trapped, which is what it feels like when you're alone with six kids. Perhaps it's the overwhelm, knowing its ferocity even when my husband is home with me. Perhaps it's much ado about nothing and I'm more competent than I think.

And perhaps, at the end of these three days, I will have surprised myself, because I will have survived. No—more than survived. Enjoyed the moments I could, forgiven the moments I failed, and laughed a whole lot.

(Epilogue: I did.)

26. Choosing Kindness Changes Us and the World

Lately I've devoted hours of time to studying fairy tales, a little research project that seems never to finish. I tend to get obsessive about things in which I'm interested. I'm reading an encyclopedia of fairy tales that spans more than 1,500 pages and includes tales from many different traditions and cultures.

One of the tales that remains relatively consistent throughout all the retellings is that of Cinderella. The story (and sometimes Cinderella) may be called something different, and the morals may point to something that lines up more with the culture in which it was told, but, for the most part, Cinderella is a story about the importance and necessity of kindness.

In some of the versions of the story I've read, Cinderella allows her stepmother and stepsisters to leave behind their limited-means way of living and live with her at the castle, returning their cruelty with extreme kindness. In some, she simply leaves them to their own lives without seeking retribution for the wrongs they did to her. In others, it is nature that has its revenge.

It's a fairy tale, but stories always have applications for our lives.

Kindness sometimes seems all too absent in our world today. We live on our computers and communicate more and more across the Internet, through social media, separated from one another in both time and space. It's much easier to be unkind to a person who isn't staring you in the face.

I've been collecting data about bullying and what it looks like in the middle school world today, because I have a story—perhaps even a series—planned that will highlight that experience and how amazing pre-teens maneuver it. I guess this, coupled with my study of fairy tales, is why kindness has been foremost in my mind lately.

We gain something from kindness. Cinderella got her prince, and we get something similar (though less…patriarchal): relationships. We learn more about people when we're kind, because people are more receptive and open to those who treat them kindly. We get to make friends, and we get to be the beneficiaries of what those people can offer us. And maybe what they offer us is not what Cinderella got from her prince—happily ever after (if that even exists)—but we are filled and healed and strengthened in community.

But the most important thing we get from being kind is identity. We are made to be kind. We are made to uplift, encourage, speak life over others. We are made to cheer one another on along the journey of life. And every time we make the choice to do so, we are solidifying our identity as kind, courageous, strong people.

It takes courage to be kind. I know. I make it my goal to be exceedingly kind wherever I go—whether I get strange or judgmental looks, whether someone makes a rude comment about me or my large family (and they do), whether I am ripped apart online for the choices I've made in life. I smile, I excuse myself, I let them get their vitriol off their chest—because kindness is about more than an interaction. It's also about the way we choose to see those people who tear us down. I choose to see them as people who are hurt or disappointed or maybe just lonely.

Exceeding kindness changes us. We begin to open to the stories and perceptions of other people, and even if they don't return our kindness, we can rest knowing that we have done our very large part of making the world a better place. We may be the only kindness they ever meet.

Cinderella got to rule a kingdom for her kindness. I wonder what we'll be asked to do.

27. Always Look for the Colors of Life

We paused beside the river, at a small shallow spot surrounded by sand. My sons kept toeing the water, walking its length, racing back out to play on the sand, build sand castles, dig a hollow in which to pour water, watch it meander and drip back to its source. My husband and I compared their shoulders, predicted which one would be broadest, tallest, most athletic.

"They are amazing creations."

Which one of us said it? I don't remember.

He put his arm around my shoulders and kissed the top of my head.

Family is a warm yellow, curled up in the chest.

28. Take Heart: The Kids Will Be Okay

I watch the two of them, one twelve, one ten, the way they interact, lean toward one another, laugh. Sometimes I am so mesmerized by my sons I can't help but stare, at the risk of being caught and asked why.

Just because, I'll say.

Just because: Because they are growing up, because they're remarkable, because I love them.

This morning I turn my back, listen to their goofing around, until my second son tells his oldest brother, "Don't get in my face. You're too close," and my chest squeezes.

My oldest son doesn't have much awareness of personal space—not much awareness of the boundaries of other people at all—so when he is talking to someone, he leans in, leans in, leans in, closer, until you feel like he might swallow you; or he follows you around, a tripping hazard; or he disregards that you were already in the middle of a conversation with someone else and keeps talking, regardless.

He's done all that since he was old enough to talk, and before I knew much about autism, I thought they were quirks that meant my son was a little more self-absorbed than other children. But no. He simply doesn't know—even after the hours of practice and instruction his father and I have given him. No —it's not that he doesn't know; it's that he doesn't notice.

And though my second son has an extra dose of emotional

intelligence and compassion, his words still squeeze my chest, because with them comes the inevitable knowledge that my firstborn son may never be able to recognize when he is standing a little too close, when he is misinterpreting something someone has said (usually in the negative), when someone is uninterested in his half-hour monologue about all the cool things he did in Minecraft today.

I've read about some parents who grieve the child they imagined they'd have before an autism diagnosis changed everything. I don't feel like I've lost anything; my son is still the same child he was at the beginning—curious, inquisitive, passionate, self-absorbed, strong-willed, sometimes inflexible, easily overwhelmed, a little bit strange (but aren't we all?). And yet when I hear his brother tell him he is standing too close to his face, a burst of sadness unsteadies me. It doesn't have as much to do with who he is as the world outside these walls of my home. His brother will treat him kindly; we have talked to all our sons about their oldest brother's challenges and capacities and how we can help him be the best version of himself he can be (which is not eliminating all signs of autism, of course, but utilizing his strengths and intentionally developing his weaknesses). My second son is doing exactly what my husband and I have always told our sons to do: Use your words.

I glance over my shoulder. My oldest son has given his brother more space, but after a few minutes, he leans too close again.

"You're too close to my face again," my second son says, and again: that same pinch in my chest.

My firstborn son is safe here, in my home, but what about out there? Already he has been teased and called terrible names for his inflexibility and the tears that come readily in certain situations. Already he has spent time in the school counselor's office after admitting to a friend that he wanted to die. Already he is having trouble distinguishing between real friends and those who are much less than. And when I think about the years ahead, my chest tightens even more. Maybe I should pull him out, protect him, homeschool him for a time, until the maturation process evens some things out—or maybe never does at all. I'm not really sure what to expect; I only have my fears and the volumes of research I've done—but even that is not entirely exhaustive. Every kid with ASD is different.

My two sons laugh together, and when I glance over my shoulder now, they're both bent over a book, sharing old Garfield comics, heads touching. I have only seconds to watch before they discover me or one of their little brothers needs me or the red snapper I'm browning in the iron skillet needs flipping. I watch for a minute anyway. My oldest son looks up, his eyes far away, then clearing.

"What?" he says, that lopsided grin beaming like a promise.

I shake my head. "Nothing," I say.

I think, *He'll figure it out.* I think, *He'll be okay.* I think, *He always has been.*

29. Learn From Each Other's Differences

Marriage has been on my mind lately—probably because this month my husband and I celebrated fourteen years of marriage.

When we married on a cloudy October day fourteen years ago, we were idealistic kids, wearing love-colored glasses that erased things like a man taking off his shoes in the middle of the house so a woman would trip on them when she wasn't looking; a woman squeezing the toothpaste from the top, rather than the bottom, because this is the only logical way; dishes left in the sink, clothes littering the floor, dinners that repeated too frequently to be considered anything but boring.

We were two different people. We came from two different backgrounds. We were raised differently, taught to value different things, shaped by our environments in different ways. We carried different victories, different wounds, different scars. We interpreted the words, actions, and motivations of people differently.

Over the years we learned, in an awkward, fumbling way, how to open ourselves to one another. We learned how not to diminish the experience of one another by explaining it away, or, worse, saying one or the other was being ridiculous for feeling this way or that way. We learned that feelings, beliefs, hopes, worries, the whole array of human emotion is valid—whether or not we readily agree with the emotions and experience of the other. We learned, most importantly, to listen to the words that lived underneath the spoken-aloud ones—the hidden words that were huddled up in balls of hurt, disappointment, fear, hopelessness. These were the most important words, because they required work to uncover them. They required patience. They required listening with both a mind and a heart.

In the work of these last fourteen years, we have uncovered my fear of abandonment, which drives my response to conflict, which drives my wall-building, which drives my sense of isolation, which drives...well, perhaps you get the picture.

A marriage of fourteen years does not flourish without listening for these places of difference, without laying love gently over them so the hardened shells begin to soften. Even after fourteen years spent together, I still do not know completely what it's like to be Ben, because I have never lived his life or grown up a boy named Ben. And he still does not know what it's like to be Rachel, because he has never lived my life or grown up a girl named Rachel. And so every day we battle our own defenses, and we seek to better and more wholly understand each other.

Because we belong to each other. Because this is what it means to love and be loved. Because the world needs more of this kind of love, stretched liberally across all the places where we are most different.

CHOICES

30. Remember: What You Do is Not Who You Are

He was playing a video game for his designated technology time, but he was crying.

I gave him a few minutes, thought maybe it would die down and he would master the game and the whine-crying would cease. But it continued.

I was trying to read a book about the adolescent brain—which was difficult enough without the interruption of an upset son, which always signals to my brain, my heart, and my body that I must turn my attention to the weeping one. This is, I suppose, the natural inclination of a mother: to heal the hurt of her children.

I put down my book and watched him. His face was already red. Tears dripped in a continuous trail down his sun-browned cheeks.

In my house, it's perfectly fine to cry. Crying is helpful and healing and completely natural. However, I find it especially perturbing when a child is crying continuously about something that is supposed to be fun; the obvious thing to do was quit playing what was making him cry.

My son had done this very same thing a couple of days ago —cried during the whole half-hour of tech time he spent on the Nintendo Switch, after which he had a headache and had to lie down.

I said, "Maybe you should put it away."

He ignored me and continued trying. I let him have another minute, torn by my desire for him to keep trying and the way his cry was snipping at my nerves. I said, "Put it away, baby. It's silly to cry about a game that's supposed to be fun. Remember what happened last time?"

He reluctantly put it away.

After a few minutes, he said, "When you said it was silly to cry about something that's supposed to be fun, were you saying I'm silly?"

I put my book down again. I explained to him that calling what he *does* silly does not mean *he* is silly.

"But it's something I do," he said.

"But what you do doesn't make who you are," I said. We've told our sons this over and over and over again, but it's a difficult concept to grasp. I said, "If I yell, does that make me a yeller?"

"No."

"If I lie, does that make me a liar?"

"Well, if you do it often enough."

I held up a finger and shook my head. "It might make me seem like a person who lies," I said. "But it doesn't make me a liar."

It's a subtle difference, with a nuance that is often lost on young children, but he is growing older, and he has heard this before. Hearing it another time will solidify it in his mind and heart and, more importantly, his identity. So I continued. I said, "'Liar' is a negative label. We don't use negative labels for people, only for actions. So you're not silly. Some things you do might be silly, but that does not make *you* silly."

He looked at me for a minute, grinned, and stood up, heading toward the playroom, where LEGOs waited for building. On his way, he pretended to walk into an invisible door. A perfect finale for such a serious talk.

31. Find the Beauty in Storms

Lightning illuminates the window, like a scary film's opening. My husband and I look at each other. We can already tell it's going to be a bad one. Which means...
Knock knock knock
It begins.
Over the next half-hour, they are in and out of our room, racing between the gaps of lighting and thunder. The rumbling crashes and echoes across the canyon in a way that makes it sound much worse than it actually is. The rain hisses and whips against the window, the wind's intensity escalating into what sounds like a dragon's roar.
They are, predictably, scared. And though the knocking followed by kids announcing they're scared (as if we don't already know) starts to get annoying when my husband and I are ready to go to bed ourselves, I know that the announcement, the communal nature of this safe place, this bedroom where a mom and dad recline with books open on their laps, is a comforting place. I remember how terrifying storms could be when I was a kid. My mom would let my sister and brother and me sleep together in the living room, which sat in the center of our house. I remember once sleeping in boxes, like we were camping in our own personal tents, but that memory might be inaccurate, something I constructed over an experience less exotic.
I used to dislike storms, and I still dislike driving in them.

When I was a teenager I used to check the clouds to make sure there were no funnels, because I was terrified of tornadoes. Now I rarely worry about that sort of thing; San Antonio is not known for tornadoes. I've grown up, and storms are, if not calming, at least tolerable. But I remember enough to empathize with my sons, so patience does not feel like it asks too much tonight (though a sleep-deprived tomorrow might tell another story).

Eventually our sons go to sleep and my husband and I lie awake in our bed, the storm roaring and flashing outside our bedroom window. Both of us toss and turn, finding sleep close to impossible.

But maybe storms are not meant to be slept through.

Maybe they are, instead, meant to be enjoyed.

I watch the lightning illuminate my window until sleep at last settles.

32. Choose Kindness and Love Always

I'm feeing a little beaten down this week. Insults and fury seem to have traded places with kindness and empathy. Sometimes I feel so discouraged by it all that I don't want to emerge from my safe shell.

But then I remember that the world needs sensitive people like me.

One of the reasons I write books (I don't often advertise this one) is because stories cultivate empathy in their readers. Empathy is becoming ever more important for this state in which we find our world today and, sadly, ever more diminished. Stories help heal that gulf between Me and Them. And readers are the ones who step into the gap.

What many in our world often forget is that no one hears us when we are mean. We become a clanging cymbal, a sounding gong, a drone in the ears of our fellow, honorable, beloved people. What we need is to torch our assumptions and stomp (or perhaps dance?) on their ashes, because they don't belong in respectful conversation. They don't belong in a loving humanity.

Here are three things I tell my sons in heated situations:

1. Take some deep breaths until you feel calmer. (If it takes days, give it days)
2. Remember who you are—strong, kind, courageous, but mostly son (or daughter).
3. Love is the whole and more than all.

My seven-year-old, yesterday, wrote words ("I have a dream that everyone will get along and be a big, happy family") on a piece of heart-shaped notebook paper. I know it's naive (I've never claimed to be anything else), but I would like to see his words become a possibility, a dream with strong, beautiful, tireless legs—but in order for that to happen, we must first let down our walls and invite others in. We must unlock our guarded hearts. We must become unafraid of being hurt, ridiculed, beaten down because of our improbable, unquenchable love.

We must learn to forgive and accept ourselves so we can learn to forgive and accept others.

"Finish each day and be done with it," said Ralph Waldo Emerson. "You have done what you could; some blunders and absurdities have crept in; forget them as soon as you can. Tomorrow is a new day; you shall begin it serenely and with too high a spirit to be encumbered with your old nonsense."

Remember who you are. Strong, kind, courageous, but mostly? You are simply son or daughter. There is nothing you have to do today or any other day to prove that you are worthy of love.

You were born worthy.

So live as though you—and others—are.

33. Don't Let Social Media Rule You

The search for significance is an endless one.

A literary magazine came in the mail today, one in which I had a silly kids' poem print, and I had to share it with the people in my writer's group. I *had* to. Why?

I don't know why. I thought maybe I was doing it just to contribute, to add a little joy to their lives, but what are the real reasons that we share these things? Is it because we are looking for validation, we are seeking likes and pleasure from other people, or is it because we really want to add something to their day's experience?

It's a slippery slope.

Social media makes it easy to bend our heads toward validation. It tricks us into thinking we need it. That's how we find worth—how many people liked what we shared?

I don't want to be dependent on others' validation. I often go weeks, sometimes even months, without checking social media because of this tendency of mine, because I know what it does to me emotionally, because I want to write without the pressure that comes from the question, *But will they like it?*

I had a poem print in a literary magazine, yes, but what you also don't see from that one little picture is that before the acceptance I got twenty-seven rejections for the same poem.

One victory amid countless defeats.

The real story happens in the living.

34. Know Your Limits and Stick Within Them

I've felt the crowding of my schedule of late.

It's the holiday season, and activities tend to pile up in what, at first, seems to be an intentional way but, once done, appears more like a large glob of frenzied activity.

I can feel out of sorts when schedules are interrupted and life starts to feel crowded. I don't like clutter—physical or otherwise—so when my calendar includes event after event after event, my defenses start lifting without my hardly even realizing. I get testy, bite out replies to perfectly reasonable questions from my children ("May I have some milk" being the most recent one).

It took me a long time to put my finger on busyness as the reason for my overwhelm and unusual temper and overall sense of doom and disappointment. I had no idea that clutter—especially when I could not really see that clutter unless I was looking for it—could make me feel so out of sorts.

My husband and I used to have a band together. We would travel around playing at youth camps and concert halls and outdoor festivals. After a while we got busy—but not quite busy enough for me to quit my full-time job. I would work all day, play concerts at night, and, when the travel moved out of the night-trip area, take my work on the road with me.

By the end of that season I had trouble getting out of bed and facing another overwhelming day. It was exhaustion, partly, but something more, too. I didn't yet know myself well enough to understand that one of my greatest needs as an introvert and a person is space.

Space in my calendar, space in my home, space in my mind.

The season ended, but life does not resolve itself so neatly; now kids compounded the busyness—activities, school projects, programs, concerts, homework, daily guidance—there is rarely an end to the demands placed on my schedule.

But over the years I have learned to carve out my space—an evening reading in my room with the door shut; excusing myself from a holiday party if the schedule-crowding proves too much activity, with little guilt (or not as much as there used to be); saying no to what I must.

I am not always good at saying no, but I do try to practice as often as I need.

After all, for a season to be embraced with joy one must also know one's limits.

35. Listen to Your Body's Wisdom

I spent a week deviating from my normal eating lifestyle, because it was my birthday, and, rather than a deviant day, I wanted a deviant week (but not a deviant month. That, I thought, was taking it too far).

It's difficult having a birthday so close to New Year's, when I renew my commitment to eating in a healthy, sustainable way. Over the course of that birthday week (actually it was, more precisely, two days), I ate an entire carton of Ben & Jerry's The Tonight Dough.

I have always had a difficult relationship with food; early anorexic behaviors turned into calorie obsession, which has, in my mothering years, turned into a healthy living obsession. So on deviant weeks, there is the significant pleasure of not worrying about calories and what I'm putting into my body and there is also the significant guilt of putting all that awful stuff into my body. It is a tension from which I can seemingly never escape—so that pleasure always feels tinged with regret, which manifests as a sharp voice of reason: "This is going to make you sick/fat/ugly/unhealthy."

It's an annoying voice to hear on a birthday week. But I live with the tension—if not gladly, then at least willingly.

Spoils of the birthday week: Two pieces of cake, one chocolate chip gourmet cookie, a carton of Ben & Jerry's The Tonight Dough, some Trader Joe's chocolate covered peppermint patties, and a couple handfuls of Trader Joe's Scandinavian Swimmers.

This week my stomach tells me I'm ready to head back into the arms of healthy choices. So I listen.

36. Edit Your Life

At the beginning of every year, I choose a word to frame my year—both the business one and the personal one. Sometimes I choose two different words to encapsulate those pieces of me. Sometimes the word is the same.

This year the word "edit" stuck out to me for both my personal life and my business life.

Edit is a word that means much to me; before I became a full-time author, I spent seven years of my professional life as a managing editor. I wrote stories, read stories, cut stories. Mostly I cut stories.

Edit, to me, is a word that means "cut" in the gentlest sense. An editor cuts unnecessary words to make something more concise and, most times, better. An editor makes important decisions about what runs in a newspaper and what needs more work or should be dismissed altogether. An editor is a shaper.

It was with this in mind that I began my year.

Business had gotten a bit out of hand. For the last three years, I have been writing daily in a notebook; this is a practice I am not willing to edit. But the practice had grown—instead of writing *one* thing a day, I had taken it upon myself to write *three*.

Which is much harder than only one, not just because of the commitment but because of the time it takes. I have a husband and young children, and they all need me. I cannot ignore them for the sake of daily writing—which, to be clear, was a practice in addition to the four hours I spent in structured writing every day. The daily writing was supposed to be a playful, fly-by-the-moment practice. It had become a burden.

Instances like these—and there were many more, as well as examples from the personal realm—underlines the importance of this word, "edit," that frames my year. I did not and do not want to burn out. I did not and do not want to produce work that is less than my best. I needed—and need—to edit.

So how it is going, halfway through the year?

Editing activities and actions and, sometimes, people takes time. That is to say, I am still in process. I do not know if I will be finished with this editing by the end of the year. A business—a life—like mine takes time to edit. Sometimes, in the process of weighing one thing over another, it can feel like I'm turning the direction of a very large ship. It demands strength and stamina and resilience and certainty.

And what of the edited pieces? How am I deciding what stays and what goes?

Goals come into play, of course. What do I want to be doing? What do I enjoy doing? What feels like a drag on my time and energy that does not really accomplish much in the way of goals and traction? What could my time be used to do, instead, that may be more effective and more enjoyable?

Who does not accept me for who I am? People who expect too much; who demand more than I can give; who tear down, rather than build up—they all take a toll on a heart and mind. And a gentle pulling away, a separation of self from what could become toxic, a brave declaration that enough is enough is sometimes in order to find our bearings again. This, too, will be under consideration.

Editing is a circle. We edit, we assess, we live, we learn, we edit.

37. Recognize, Accept, and Restrain the Darkness Within

Around Christmas time one year, when my oldest son was four or so, someone asked him if he'd been good this year. It was an innocent question, a question people often ask children because it is, in the folklore of contemporary life, tied to the gifts that might be waiting underneath the tree come Christmas morning.

My son was never one for masks and pretending. He said, "I've been a little good and a little bad."

And it was true; he had.

(At least, he'd made both good and bad choices; my husband and I don't assign "good" or "bad" to people.)

This contradiction lives in all of us. We all have the capacity within us to be a hero one day and a villain the next. We all have a measure of good that is countered by a measure of evil (though we are not, ourselves, *good* or *evil*; we are simply human). We all wrestle with both light and darkness.

I want, more than anything, to be kind in all ways. I desire to make every interaction count. I hope, always, to be an ever-present, encouraging voice.

And yet there are times I feel myself overcome with emotion—so overcome that my greatest desire is to lash out and hurt, to say words that I know I'll regret later, to feel the power, however convoluted or corrupt it is, of being on top for just a moment in time.

There is a mean bone in all of us that wants to feel like we matter in the grand scheme of things, that we belong somewhere, that we are people who have a small pinch of power.

These contradictions that exist within all of us are relatively harmless—when our thoughts remain thoughts and we remain vigilant. When we recognize, accept, and restrain them.

In these contradictions, we can feel the connection of humanity—the dark impulses rising up in us that we can imagine rise up in everyone else, too. If we sit with that darkness for a while, we can understand the impulses that govern the cruel; we can measure the capacity for harm; we can almost, maybe just a little bit, fathom why this hatefulness sometimes spills out into the fraught spaces of the world.

But if we deny these dark places within ourselves, if we say of course we have never had a terrible thought about another person, if we do not at least momentarily acknowledge and connect with that side of ourselves, we will never completely understand the failures of some to control it.

And, what is more, when our darkness is ignored and denied as though it never existed at all, it becomes stronger and more difficult to control.

If ignored and denied long enough, we could fall into the gap between our real selves and our imagined (better) selves. And once in the gap, the darkness does not have to work hard to best our control, to control *us* instead of the other way around.

Better to deny or acknowledge?

I know which I'd choose.

38. Live an Uninhibited Life

There is a boy in my home who moves effortlessly through the world.

When I say effortlessly, it is not to say that everything comes easily for him. He works hard at math and sometimes gets stuck on a vocabulary word, but effortlessly, in his case, means unbound and uninhibited.

He is a boy I will watch, mesmerized, as he breaks out into the silliest dance you've ever seen just to make everybody in the room laugh. He is a boy who will blow dramatic kisses, and, when I return them, mime all sorts of obstacles standing in the way between him and that floating-away kiss, making him look like an American Ninja Warrior in training. He is a boy who will turn a succession of forward flips all the way from his room to mine, to say goodnight, and then turn around and do the same all the way back to bed, because he just thought it would be fun.

He is the most uninhibited person I have ever known.

The other day, as he came in to tell me good night, he pretended like he was a zombie, turning his voice airy and squeezed up tight so I could better know what he was emulating. I laughed so hard. He makes my night.

What I love about all of this is that my son doesn't care in the least what other people think. He moves through his world being who he is, and it doesn't matter to him, at least not yet, if others think he's strange or silly or a big clown. He is completely comfortable with who he is, and I know he's only seven, but there's so much I can learn from him.

Once we become aware of ourselves, we can't forget ourselves. I have been aware of myself for a long time. I know I'm a sensitive person who will cry at the least little thing because life affects me profoundly. I know that at any given time in the course of a conversation or an interaction with another person, I have at least two storylines running in my head, and my brain is recording every single tiny detail so I can use it later. I know that when my husband forgets to text me when he gets somewhere he's traveled, it can set up a whole current of anxiety that will carry me into a deep, black hole.

Sometimes I have apologized for these things I know about myself. *I'm sorry I cry so much. I'm sorry I missed that thing you said because I was creating a fictional world in my head. I'm sorry I freak out about everything.*

What my seven-year-old has taught me is that we must, instead, embrace who we are. We must move more like children —unbound, uninhibited, unapologetic about all the weird and quirky traits we have. Our weirdness is what makes this world hilarious and interesting and even (Oh! Could it be true?) beautiful.

Here's what happens when you choose to live an uninhibited life:

You begin to feel less limited, as if there are endless possibilities for who you are—not a single, neat, taped-up box.

You begin to understand that other people have their own quirks, and when you embrace yours, they have freedom to embrace theirs.

You begin to love yourself. And that will impact every other area in your life.

I have a post-it note stuck to my mirror, where I write every day at a makeshift standing desk. It says, "Be yourself, in kindness, in courage, and in love." That post-it note reminds me to embrace who I am and live fearlessly.

Go be yourself, in kindness, in courage, and in love.

39. Assert Yourself

At the close of every year, I always find myself turning my gaze to the new year—sometimes even before it's time.

There are certainly times in which to begin anew—the beginning of a summer, a birthday, an anniversary, the start of a school year. But there is no time that lends itself to new beginnings quite like a new year. It's a wide open opportunity that meets each of us with a clean slate, a schedule that hasn't yet filled with activities (unless you have school children). We aren't on the hook for projects to deliver or goals we've set and still need to meet. Everything is expansive and rich with potential.

If you want to make a drastic change in direction, a new year is the perfect time to do it.

Sometimes that can be an unsettling thing, like a writer facing a blank page for the first time, which is pretty much any time, because there is no formula for writing. So much space and possibility can feel intimidating to some.

I get giddy with anticipation. I evaluate and schedule and write down goals and revise goals and decide on publication dates for self-published books and mark dates for traditionally published books and plan for the projects on which I'd like to focus for the coming year and try to anticipate the bumps I might meet in the road (though I can't always predict those with any accuracy.). I analyze daily writing expectations, manage those expectations, strip everything away and add it back. I brainstorm new ideas and white board and think, think, think. I assess my schedule and see if it still works for me.

One of my most important goals this year is to better assert myself.

Assertion is not one of my strengths. When faced with a decision to assert my needs that come in conflict with another's needs, I will generally default to the other person's needs. This could be the result of residual trauma from my past, or it could simply be a weakness of mine cultivated in my childhood quest to demand the least attention, step on the fewest toes, be the "easiest" child. But what I have learned of weakness is that when we recognize it, examine it, and intentionally practice strengthening it, it will not remain a weakness for long.

This last year I encountered several instances in which I needed to assert myself in order to make sure my needs were met in a timely and efficient manner. Instead, I chose the least resistant path—that of acquiescence and accommodation.

Assertion is an important part of communication when you work for yourself and you depend on other people for your ultimate success. Asking for what you want and need is necessary for healthy relationships, successful careers, and even enduring marriages.

I don't yet know for what I will ask in this new year, at least not completely. But I do know that when I stumble into a situation that calls for assertion, I will be (mostly) ready to stumble through it (we all start somewhere) and, by the end of the year, walk through it with my head held high.

40. Let the Optimism of Kids Become Your Own

We celebrate the end of the school year with ice cream. During the eating, we talk about braces, plans for the summer, creative projects my sons want to do, books they want to read. Their attention wanders, my husband and I guide it back. They admire the bright pictures of other people's ice cream choices —"Hey, that one has gummy worms like mine!" "Ew, orange sherbet with strawberries?" "What kind of ice cream is that?" We remind them to use their indoor voices.

Back at home, my sons act silly through our reading time, brushing teeth time, and going to bed time, their little bodies thrumming with the foreign sugar invading their systems. They love us for letting them have a treat, and then they hate us for making them go to bed—the emotions a vacillating axe ready to fall on whatever extreme it can. I worry they're never going to sleep, worry they're going to get cavities, worry about all the bills that still need to be paid. They worry about what they're going to do tomorrow—can they have ice cream again?

Certainly not. (This I don't say aloud.)

"I think the twins have optimism," my second son says, out of the blue, on his way out of the bathroom. I don't know what they were discussing. My thoughts carried me away for a moment.

My husband gives them all a test for optimism—asks them if they all think we'll have a good day tomorrow. They all say yes

(some louder than others). Especially if they get ice cream again.
(Certainly not.)
Majority rule. So I believe it will be a good day, too.

41. What Doesn't Bring Joy Doesn't Belong

I quit social media.

I didn't really quit social media. I've just taken some time away from it, after considering how much time I could devote to other things—laundry or cutting up lettuce or even showering.

I didn't spend all that much time on social media in the first place; I cheated with a scheduling service that posted at periodic times, and every now and then I'd log in and see if I needed to respond to any comments or tags. So the falling away didn't feel all that drastic. It felt mostly natural. After living for so long completely overwhelmed by the necessity of being in so many places at one time—all those social platforms the professionals said I needed to use if I was going to see success as an author—and after trying to maintain a fun and consistent presence in those places for a significant amount of time, I finally burned myself out enough to disappear. I started with a month-long social media fast; it ended with a slow, long avoidance.

It feels mostly good. I don't have to post things to find affirmation. The people with whom I want to maintain contact are still in my life; we text, we see each other in person, we talk on the phone, we email. I haven't lost anything more than a platform on which to talk about me or my children—which I can do without.

During the fast, at the time of my overwhelm, I finally decided that not everyone in the world should have access to my life or the lives of my husband and children. I still write blogs; if people are interested in the things I am learning or what's going on in my life, they can read those. I send out a monthly newsletter; those who are curious about what's going on in both my professional and personal life (as well as book recommendations and peeks inside my writing projects) can sign up for that. I don't need to live a public life when I am a private individual. I need time away.

My disappearance coincides with my significant journey toward health and fitness, which has resulted in a forty-pound loss and a return to the weight of my pre-children, college days. Sometimes I miss social media when I think about the victory of that and how my journey might inspire someone else. But is it altruism that would drive me to post about the forty pounds lost through intermittent fasting and running six or more daily miles, or the ego's constant craving for validation?

I think we probably all know the answer to that. And so I remain invisible, anonymous, un-congratulated—a place that, once there, you realize isn't all that bad.

42. Lose the Apologetic Tone

Some of my fellow writers congregated in an online group, talking about how they are always hogging attention from the agent we share, begging her to pay attention to them. Another of them confessed that he was much too shy for that sort of thing, and maybe he should take a page out of their book, so to speak.

I clung to the background, as I typically do even in online conversations. I like to listen more than I talk and only weigh in when I feel I have something valuable to say.

The problem is, I can often convince myself that I don't have anything valuable to say.

At first, I agreed with the writer who called himself shy, though I would never use that particular term for myself. But as I considered my reluctance to "demand attention," as I thought about the messages I send to my agent or my editor or, really, any fellow writer, I realized that it is not shyness that inhibits me, it is fear—fear of being an inconvenience, fear of being seen as annoyingly needy, fear of overstepping some invisible boundary I've set for myself.

Most of my correspondence with professional people in my industry can be described with one word: apologetic. Sometimes I say the words, *I'm sorry*. Sometimes I don't—but regardless, the tone always implies that I am apologetic for requiring even a moment of extra time or thought or consideration.

I could trace the fear, I'm sure, back to something in my childhood. My mother was a single mother for a significant period of my life: I was a Second Mom. I did everything I could to make life a little smoother for her; I did not want to require more than she could give. I often buried my needs under a blanket of Everything's Fine. Women and girls learn to do that early in life, don't they?

This burial practice has followed me into most of my relationships. I find it agonizing to ask for help when I need it. I don't like burdening people with my small and unimportant (in my mind) problems. I will spend a week reading and re-reading the email I've already revised thirty times, asking a question in that same apologetic way, before hitting send.

I see how this has limited my engagements and impacted my relationships. I have little knowledge how to change it.

But perhaps recognition is the starting line; perhaps seeing clearly is what it takes before a change can even become possible. Because the next time I craft an email, I will consciously eliminate the apologetic tone and delete every instance of "sorry."

A word I've already said too many times in my life.

43. Never Let the Opinions of Others Silence You

The other night, my husband and I watched *Dead Poet's Society*, a movie I remember loving in high school. I loved it just as much this time around. It is a phenomenal movie with phenomenal writing and acting.

But.

It struck me differently this time around. I'm a parent now. I cried—no, I sobbed—great, heaving sobs—when a boy is so beat down by the box his parents put him in—telling him who they expect him to be; what his career choice will be; what he absolutely cannot do, which happens to be his passion—that he has little freedom to enjoy his life and be who he is. He feels stuck in a future of his parents' making, and it holds nothing he wants or needs.

As a parent, I cannot see this movie without feeling the weight of this responsibility: to let my children be who they are, not who I want them to be.

It's one of the most important things in the world. It's the way we show them love. It's how we teach them to be themselves—and not anybody else's definition of who they should be.

We all maneuver through a time when the thoughts and opinions of other people mean something to us, whether those "other people" are our parents or our friends or our spouses or our brothers and sisters. Maybe those thoughts and opinions will always mean something to us, because we're relational people.

But oh!—we should never, ever let them limit us.

When I was in college, I was. 4.0 student, but I got a B in my first creative writing class. In fact, my professor so disliked my poetry (he called it florid and melodramatic) that he scrawled on one of my assignments something along the lines of, "Probably not a future for you here in poetry." He said pretty much the same about my fiction (he was not a nice person).

On Sept. 18, 2018, *The Colors of the Rain*, a novel written entirely in poetry, was published by a reputable New York publishing house.

I thought about sending him a copy but, in the end, I didn't. Why waste the postage? And the complimentary copy? He didn't really deserve the courtesy.

I let my professor's words stifle me for a while. I put down my fiction and poetry pen and picked up my journalism one. I wouldn't change that choice, knowing what I know today, but I would change the way I let him bully me out of my dream, which was always to be a poet and a novelist. I thought, then, that the things people said about me defined me. They knew more about me than I did, I believed. They could see things I couldn't. They were right.

They didn't, they couldn't, and they weren't.

"They" can't say what you get to be or who you are or even why you were put here on this earth. We aren't made for someone else's box. We are made for something far greater: our purpose. And only we can know that.

I have been called many things in my life, some of them unthinkable, some of them moderately annoying—for writing what I write, for choosing to have six children, for speaking out against judgment and hate. I have never let these dishonorable, sometimes vile, always highly inaccurate names define me, impede my vision, or silence me from speaking what I must speak.

Neither should you.

Be your wondrous, brave, spectacular self. Today and every day.

LAUGHTER

44. Find Humor in the Hardest Places

They were rowdy, loud, and I hadn't quite gotten enough sleep last night. The noises were grating on me: some kids shrieking (at least it was in happiness, or something close to it), another kid tapping the table with a spoon (a soundtrack rhythm of annoying proportions), and one more kid racing a scooter through the kitchen (adding to the shrieks), while I tried to put together a smoothie for breakfast.

I poured the yogurt, shook out strawberries, added a few frozen bananas and switched on the blender, enjoying the familiar hum that almost drowned out the sounds of my children. I closed my eyes, trying not to count how many summer days remained, trying to breathe and grasp at a flimsy, slippery hope, trying not to admit that this—this intolerable, madness-filled morning—was the last straw of summer vacation.

I shut off the blender. Turned toward the glasses, lined up. Started to pour.

Someone screeched.

"This is the last straw."

Had I said the words aloud?

I looked up. My oldest son was staring at me, his brown eyes wide. He repeated himself. "This is the last straw." He held out a mason jar, one stainless steel straw scraping along its lip.

"Where are the other straws?" he said.

I couldn't answer. I could only laugh.

He stared at me for a minute, then bent and opened the dishwasher, where other straws gathered in one rectangular tray. He stuck them in the cups after I filled them.

I thanked him for his help—a bright spot in an otherwise trying span of moments.

45. Accept the Gifts Others Give

During a recent Sunday, as my family and I sat waiting for a luncheon to begin, an older man sat beside me and said all the things my husband and I have come to expect from people who observe and comment on our family—six kids—we know how it happens, don't we? my goodness they're all boys???, how do you do it? But he was an older man, which means instead of asking, "You're done now, right?" like the younger ones tend to do, he asked, "So do you want a boy or a girl next?"

After laughing through the answer to that question (an adamant, "No more for me!"), the man went on and on about my sons' good manners. They were in excellent form this particular day; if he'd seen them at the dinner table last night he would have thought the complete opposite, several of them chewing with their mouths hanging open so wide I'm surprised they didn't drop all their food on the floor—and there was plenty of it there without the help of their open mouths. Sometimes, in fact, I wonder if good manners even exist in the Possible Things Boys Can Have, but this man seemed to think they did.

Well, then.

They are all so well behaved for a brood so big and boyish, he continued, and we chatted until it was time to feed the hungry pack and he left to find his wife and table. My husband went off to grab lunch plates for all of us, while I wrestled my sons into their seats so they didn't look like uncivilized wildlings after receiving so many compliments (sometimes compliments put more pressure on you, don't they? To maintain? To be what they think you are? To pretend that you have it all together and are doing just fine?).

While my husband was gone, the man sat back down in the lone empty chair at the table and pulled out his wallet and said, "I bet you'd like to send your boys to camp or something this summer." I said a hasty, "Yes, sure," even though my husband and I aren't really camp people. The man took out two fifty-dollar-bills and placed them in my hands and said, "I just wanted to give you this, and I don't want to offend you or anything. I know you don't need charity, but I just felt like I needed to."

I thanked him profusely, unsure momentarily what to do. I could give him a book or two, I could offer an edit for a really short composition, I could do any number of things—but he was giving that money just to give, and who was I to deny him the delight of that? I know the joy that comes from giving when we have the means to give, the way it fills us up much more than an account full of money could ever do. So I have learned, in my life, to accept those gifts gratefully.

Before he left, the man said, "I really heard God tell me to give you two hundred and fifty dollars, but I didn't want to do that."

I laughed about his honesty all the way home.

46. Treasure the Ironic Moments

It's always perplexing to me that my ten-year-old can spend hours arranging and rearranging his LEGO creations, taking pictures, making stop motion videos, a tedium I think I would have little patience for seeing through, and yet when it comes to chores—sweeping a fifteen-foot-by-fifteen-foot room—his leg is hurting or his toe feels like it might fall off or his arm—the whole thing, yes—has not yet recovered fully from some earlier (invisible) injury.

47. Embrace Your Childlike Nature

On our way home from dropping their brothers off at the elementary school down the road, my twins always run ahead of me to collect some sticks. They like to use these sticks as magic wands, with which they will point at people and gleefully yell, "Exsmelliarmpits," a word we came up with as a fun twist on the Harry Potter magical term, *Expelliarmus*.

They do this with such gusto, without apology, without worrying about what the people on the other end of the make-believe spell will think of them. And most of the time those people laugh.

What I see in them is bravery—to be who they are. What I see is invention and play. What I see are some lessons I should take to heart:

1. Own it—your silliness, your fun, your childlike nature
2. Be unafraid to move in the world as you are
3. Make something your own

This is how we live a creative life.

48. Laugh at Yourself

My family and I went to a haunted trail yesterday, and I have discovered that what I once considered my strong constitution is, in fact, considerably weak. It can only take so much before it quivers and folds.

We walked through woods, where people in masks—clowns, rabid pandas, creepy human-sized dolls—hid, waiting for unsuspecting passersby before leaping out from the trees. It sounds milder than it was, I'm sure. I gripped the right hand of my husband and the left hand of my seven-year old, who said, periodically, "I'm going to have nightmares"—and yet he continued on, so I continued on. (If he had quit, I'm fairly certain I would have, too. But surely I am at least as brave as a seven-year-old.)

We continued past creepy dolls with knives, terrifying children (who are often the most frightening sights of all, in the dark) with stringy hair combed over their faces, and ghostly figures that thrust sound makers in our faces, every click and snap making me jump.

I screamed at practically every turn.

My sons are still talking about my screams. They will be talking about them for days—maybe even months.

"Do you want to go again?" they said when we finally, blessedly, made it out alive.

"No," I said.

They laughed.

Hearing my sons laugh and bond at my expense almost made the terror worth it.

Almost.

EMOTIONS

49. Accept Your Neuroses With Compassion

The other day, I examined my five-year-old's head, because I'd noticed some flakes in his hair, which generally indicates either gastronomical distress or mental distress. While inspecting the dry patches, I noticed a spot that looked like a mole but was much darker than the other moles on his body—a spot I'd never noticed before, which meant it had probably popped up recently.

I should preface this by saying that I know way more about moles than the average person probably should. This is because I'm a mole-y person, and just after my second son was born (and, consequently, after I saw an episode of *Grey's Anatomy* where Izzie discovered a cancerous mole on her back, which turned into a brain tumor, which turned into…well, I don't know because I had to quit watching; my anxiety couldn't take it), I went through a postpartum paranoia about all the moles on my body. This was exacerbated by a dermatologist who seemed to sense my fear and used it to drain us of a lot of insurance and out-of-pocket money. He removed eight moles on two visits—only one of which needed further treatment.

So when I saw this spot on my son's head, I immediately freaked out. I had a full-blown panic attack in the hallway of my church, because I couldn't keep my anxious thoughts in check. My throat closed up, my knees buckled a little, and my heart started pounding like it thought I was in mortal danger.

This is what living with anxiety is like.

I took him and his brothers to the church nursery and immediately searched his twin brother's head. So the nursery workers didn't think I was looking for lice, I told them I'd found a weird spot on his twin brother and I just wanted to make sure he didn't have a spot, too. We got into a discussion about anxiety. One of the nursery workers has a teenage daughter who has frequent anxiety attacks, but she herself has never had one.

This got me wondering what it was like to live without anxiety.

My husband is the kind of person who can notice something, file it away in the back of his mind, and carry on in his normal, unaffected way. Contrast that with me: I will notice something—a checking account that isn't as full as it needs to be, someone looking at me weird, a spot on my son's scalp—and it will result in a sleepless night.

What would it be like to live without anxiety?

When we got home, I told my husband I wished I could be more like him. And he said, "But I like you as you are, anxiety and all."

And it's true. He does.

So much of the time, when we notice these "unacceptable" things about ourselves—our propensity toward pessimism or drama or anxiety or depression or manic behavior—we think it means we are less than normal, less than deserving (of anything), less than lovable. But we're not. These things don't define who we are; they're just neuroses. We are not defined by our neuroses.

So what if the deep waters of anxiety pull me down every now and then? I am not defined by my anxiety. And, more importantly, I always find my way back to the surface.

Rather than hide our quirks, we should uncover them. There is freedom here, in the honesty of being who we are, fully and unreservedly. And we never know who's watching or listening or withering in their own way, who might need the strength of our, "Sure, I've spent the last six months depressed, but I'm still here and I still deserve love and compassion." Who knows whose life we might save by being ourselves—neuroses and all.

(Epilogue: The doctor reports that the spot on our son's head is merely a normal skin spot. No need for another minute of anxiety—at least not for that problem. The hundreds of others, well…)

50. It's Okay to Acknowledge the Wound

Today I watched a woman with her daughter, spinning round and round in the neighborhood pool, and I felt the familiar ache I often feel when I see a woman with a daughter. The ache that whispers, *I wanted that, too.*

Both of them laughed. The mother pretended to toss the girl into the air, causing a squeal of delight. My stomach clenched, and a soft longing uncurled in my chest. It's a longing I know will always be present, a longing for the daughter I did not have, for the daughter I never got to meet, for the daughter who died.

She is not as tangible as she used to be in our house, when my oldest son would sometimes mention her. He is the only one who remembers what happened, the only one who knew the devastation of endings that should have been beginnings. Now months pass without a mention of her.

We try to remember, every July 1, the day of her death. But life moves on at breakneck pace, and sometimes she doesn't cross my mind until I see a mother with her daughter in the pool, spinning.

My eyes wandered back to the pair. It is interesting to observe the relationship between a mother and her daughter. Sometimes it is even healing to wonder what my relationship with my daughter would have been like, had it been given a chance to bloom.

And yet.

And yet I cannot watch their interaction without that longing. There is something missing from my life. For a long while I denied that—I had my sons; I had everything I'd ever desired.

Did I say it for them or for me?

I would not trade any of my sons' lives for a daughter; that much is certain. But a daughter would have rounded out an already-full life. The wound of losing one—it's never completely gone, no matter how much love and joy fills a life.

The little girl asked her mother to do it again, toss her again. And the mother did. And they played the game two, three, twelve more times. I smiled, and my sons came galloping toward me, spraying water everywhere. I handed them their towels and kissed their wet heads.

By the time we left the pool, the mother and her daughter were gone, like shadows dispersed by the sun.

51. Let Yourself Be Depressed, But Don't Stay There

April was probably one of the hardest months I've survived as far as mental health is concerned. My emotions were all over the place—anger, fear, anxiety, despair. And they were intense. I almost died from the flu (not really. I did have the flu, but I didn't almost die. I just like to be dramatic), I couldn't get out of bed for two days, I worried incessantly about anything and everything.

And then May came in fanfare and celebration: I had an essay print on Upworthy, I met some amazing new writer friends, I published a book, Mother's Day came and went, and I sold my first middle grade manuscript to a traditional publisher.

Some observations:

1. Emotions don't last forever. You find yourself in a slump, you'll get out of it.

2. You can handle more than you think.

3. There's nothing wrong with being down in the dumps.

4. You have to get back up. Life is too beautiful—too surprising—to miss.

52. Don't Let the Worry Spiral Win

He is late.

He usually calls or texts when he's going to be late, but lately we've been more strangers than lovers, passing each other in the hallways, smiling, dropping quick kisses, breezing out the door.

He didn't even tell me where he was going today.

I've been working on a memoir about meeting the woman who broke up my parents' marriage, along with her two kids—my half-brother and half-sister—who were kept a secret from my mother during my parents' marriage, except for the answering machine message I still remember, forever imprinted on my nine-year-old brain.

I've been dreaming about my mother, feeling her humiliation, sweating drops of regret. Today I could be her for the worry and fear that wraps around my throat and squeezes.

My thoughts seesaw between the two: What if he's with someone else? What if something happened to him?

Both are equally irrational; this has happened before when he's going to be late and he forgets to call and I work myself into an agitated state and call him a few times, text him a few times, look up every highway he might have taken today to see if there were any fatal accidents reported…and if there were, I panic even more and make irrational lists of police department numbers I can call if it gets too late and he's still not home.

And then the door opens and it's him. Standing. Smiling.

Bending to kiss me. My tears are embarrassing then, as are the messages I've left on his cell to call me, I'm worried, is he still alive? As though he could answer if he weren't.

He's also never given me any reason to believe he would be unfaithful, but when you grow up with the trauma of learning your dad—the man you trusted to love you—has a whole secret family you didn't know about, you grow up knowing anyone in the world can let you down. Anyone.

Even him.

I search for his location on my "locate iPhone" map. He's right down the road. I remember now: the workout, the business lunch. It's a good sign that he's late.

I breathe. I survive. I overcome.

One more victory against the past that likes nothing more than to strangle the present.

Not today, I whisper.

And, as if he knows exactly what I'm thinking, my husband texts, "I saved you half my sandwich. Thought you might like it for lunch."

It's divine.

53. Recognize the Gifts When They Come, However Small

I was at the eye doctor because I'd noticed a weird fleck in my eye. The fleck led me to notice an increase in floaters that have been present in my eyes for a long time but that have surely increased of late.

This is what anxiety does: It latches onto something and calls it bad. Worse. Probably you're-going-to-die proportions—and that's without the Google search.

It sends you to the doctor.

The eye doctor swept into the dim-lit examination room, where I'd dozed off in the minutes after the assistant had left. She began my exam, asked me questions. I laid out my troubles: dry eyes, vision gets blurry sometimes, read a lot. She asked me more questions—do I work on a computer? (Yes, for about five hours a day.) Do I read a lot? (Yes, more than five hours a day.) Do I ever rest my eyes? (Rest? What does that mean?)

She thought it was just my reading and writing habits. Maybe some eye drops would help.

I asked more questions, mentioned the gray square—a blind spot—that showed up three years ago. She didn't see anything on the tests. So it was…nothing? She shrugged. At least nothing to worry about.

Then she told me a story about her sister, who had noticed

that one of her eyes had brighter vision than the other. "We're kind of hypochondriacs," she said and laughed.

And immediately, just like that, I felt better. I'd found a person like me—and she was a doctor! It was almost a sort of normalcy, this hypochondria. She normalized it, because she was a doctor and she felt it, too.

Everything checked out okay, and I went on my way, certain that she will be my ophthalmologist forever.

Birds of a feather stick together.

54. Let Yourself Feel What You Feel

We've had a string of rainy days, and my sons have been cooped up in our house with little to do (so they say; they just want to make a case for more technology time. They still don't seem to understand that their father and I know the value of boredom.). Every other minute, it seems, I am diffusing fights, smoothing over tensions, and crawling my desperate way back to thankfulness.

It is an ongoing struggle; this is not the first time I have written about my failure to feel thankful in the midst of challenging circumstances, which frequently include the presence of my children. It's not that I am ungrateful for being a mother —at times I am filled with such unspeakable joy that my heart feels too large for my chest. My sons provide me a window into hope and courage and delight. I would never ever trade that.

The moments, though, sometimes crowd out that reality. The moments sometimes tell me a one-sided story: namely, that I have made a lamentable mistake in having so many. The doubts don't remain for long, however, before one of them stoops to help his brother tie his shoe, before another shares a piece of toast with the littlest, before one throws his arms around my waist and says, "I love you, Mama," so loud it's as though he wants the whole world to hear. A declaration.

The doubts, the frustrations, the second-guessing, the wonderings, the fears, the trials, the ungrateful moments—they will come again, because they are a normal part of motherhood.

But I know, too, that they always give way to the kind of moment steeped so greatly in joy that they seem transcendent.

I watch my sons join one another at the table, playing an amicable game of Monopoly—at least until someone buys a property another wants.

Trial and joy, intermingling.

55. Roll With the Punches of Anxiety

5 stories of Anxiety

1. He didn't come home when he said he would.
Neurotypical thought process:
(a) He probably got caught up with something.
(b) He's fine. He'll be home soon.
Anxiety's thought process:
(a) He hasn't called, and he's not home.
(b) He's probably dead on the side of the road.
(c) I'll need to find a job that pays enough money to support all my kids as a single mom.
(d) Oh, God.
(e) Why hasn't he called?

2. There's a strange mole on my five-year-old's head.
Neurotypical thought process:
(a) That's weird. I'll mention it to the doctor next time we go in.
(b) I'll make an appointment Monday. He'll be fine.
Anxiety's thought process:
(a) That's never been there before.
(b) It's really dark. It's probably melanoma.
(c) I need to take him to a doctor right now. Emergency room?

(d) Oh, God.

(e) What if he dies?

3. It smells a little like fire in here.

Neurotypical thought process:

(a) It's probably the heater turning on. We haven't used it in a while.

(b) Everything is fine.

Anxiety's thought process:

(a) What's that smell?

(b) The house is burning down!

(c) We need to evacuate!

(d) Oh, God!

(e) Why didn't I review the fire escape plan with them before they all fell asleep?

4. She didn't email me back.

Neurotypical thought process:

(a) She's probably gone for the weekend.

(b) It's fine.

Anxiety's thought process:

(a) Did I do something wrong?

(b) I bet she doesn't want to be my agent anymore.

(c) I need to send her another email.

(d) Oh, God.

(e) What if this is the end of my career?

5. My Honda Odyssey groans and shakes while shifting a gear.

Neurotypical thought process:

(a) It's not like it hasn't done strange things before.
(b) It's most likely nothing. It'll be fine.

Anxiety's thought process:

(a) What was that?
(b) The van feels like it's about to die!
(c) We won't have anything to drive to work, which means…
(d) Oh, God.
(e) We will never, ever, ever recover from this. Ever.

56. Keep Hope an Ever-Present Companion

After my first traditionally published book released in September 2018, once the dust settled, I felt depressed and out of sorts. Part of it could be explained away by the demands on my time and the fact that I am an introvert who gets somewhat annoyed when my schedule is interrupted with out-of-the-ordinary activity. When my calendar gets crammed, as it tends to get during a book launch season, I feel stressed and overwhelmed (which is also why my sons have not yet joined sports, though I have one in orchestra this year).

At the same time, lists began to greet me at every turn—favorite books, best books for the holidays, best-of 2018, awards lists. There is a book list for practically everything. And comparison loves lists. I fell hard into the sticky web of *I guess I'm just not good enough*.

But it was, of course, more than that.

The writing life isn't an easy one. It's especially not easy when you're the mother of young children. At the same time I was recuperating from the busy launch season I had a son struggling with middle school, another upset about the necessity of speech lessons, and two others who were having behavioral issues at school.

When there are crises in my home, my first now-predictable response, as a mother, is to question whether I am doing the right thing to pursue a career and work outside the home (even though I technically work from home). Maybe it's because of the pressures that exist in modern motherhood, but when my sons struggle, I can't help but think it's a direct reflection on the time I spend doing anything other than caring for my family.

I know I was made for writing. When I write, I feel as though I am doing exactly what I was brought into this world to do. I feel free and hopeful and alive. When I'm talking about writing or new projects or ideas I feel shaky with the bound-up energy of this knowing.

What would happen if I gave that up?

I know what would happen. I know I would not be the best version of myself that I could be. I would not fulfill my full purpose. I would waste potential and talent and opportunity. I would lament and resent.

Around this time, my husband and I prepared to visit New York for the first time, a late fifteen-year anniversary celebration of sorts. He had a work conference, I was set to meet both my agent and my editor in real life, and we had planned a day to ourselves, for pleasure and touristy things. I didn't even know if we could afford the trip in terms of both money and absence from our children, but there it was, already booked.

So I went. I had a lovely visit with my editor, who told me she absolutely loves my work and wants as much from me as she can possibly get. And the hope began to peer in at the edges.

At all junctures of my life I can feel hope peering in, no matter how bad things got. My parents divorced—there was hope. My father left in totality—there was hope. My sons and I are struggling with anxiety and depression—there is hope.

Hope is a powerful force, the kind of force that can lift our heads and whisper, *Get up, you're still alive, you were made for more than this.*

You were made for more than this burden you carry, this disappointing setback, this scary circumstance. There is still hope.

So many people in our world think and feel that they are without hope. It is up to us—the hope-filled ones (at least today)—to find them and tell them: Life's an unpredictable thing. It can change in a moment. The night never lasts forever.

RESPONSIBILITY

57. Keep a Tender Heart and a Fierce Constitution

The other night, after kids had been put to bed and my husband and I finally had a moment to ourselves, we found ourselves circling my latest burden, trying not to pinpoint it directly. It felt a little dangerous. We talked around the message I feel I have been given to share—one of love and nonviolence and hope and belonging to yourself and showing up and being you. But even while we talked around it, my eyes got blurry, my throat tight.

I could not even talk *around* it without crying.

And I finally had to say, "Sometimes it feels like there is too much asked of me. I'm tired of getting beaten up. Maybe I don't want to do it anymore."

Because it's true; sometimes I don't. I don't want to be out there in the public eye, heralding hope and justice and love and dignity for all people, only to be blasted by those who disagree with the basic tenets of humanity.

He looked at me carefully, gauging my emotional stability, feeling around in my heart, assessing the words I'd just said to determine whether or not I meant them. He said, "Your message is important."

"I know," I said.

"To a lot of people."

"I know."

"You have too much love for people to let your message go unheard. To stop using your voice." He turned me around to face him.

He said, "You're brave."

He said, "You're strong."

He said, "You're adaptable but resilient."

There is a paradoxical space between taking a stand and yet remaining pliable. Standing for something brings you to a place where you must cultivate both a tender heart and a fierce constitution. What this means, for me, is that I must remain, always, rooted in love—doing what I do, speaking what I speak, writing what I write in love, with love, for love—and yet I must shore myself up with courage and strength for the firestorm that will follow my message.

I must see the people, not the ideas those people keep. I must respond, not react. I must put on my love and wrap it around myself as tightly as is needed, tying enough knots so it never slips off. This is keeping a tender heart.

And yet I must draw boundaries around myself, to say *you do not have access to me here, where you are trying to hurt my heart*. I must stand strong against the criticism and judgment that hurtles my way. I must believe in what I say, and even if it is the kind of message I'd rather run away from and leave others to speak—I must stand up and speak.

If we cannot remain tender, we risk losing our greatest treasure: love. And if we cannot remain fierce, we risk losing our greatest asset: our identity.

May we hang on, desperately, ferociously, tenaciously to both.

58. Admit that You Don't Know Everything

If you ever want to know how much you don't know, just spend about a minute with a kid.
Do you think there were rattlesnakes in the water?
—*No. Water moccasins, maybe.*
Are they poisonous?
—*Yes.*
Do they just bite you if you're in the water, or do they have to have a reason?
—*I think if you disturb the nest they'll bite you* [This information comes from an episode of "Lonesome Dove" that I remember my mom watching when I was a child. I was slightly traumatized by it. I have since learned that water moccasins do not actually nest in water.]
Where do they nest—in the shallow water or the deep end?
—*I don't know.*
How many nest together?
—*I don't know.*
Do they have families?
—*I don't know.*
Can you describe them to me?
How long does it take them to have babies?
How many babies do they have?
Do they lay eggs?
Are the eggs waterproof?

Turns out, I don't know very much at all.

59. Embrace Your Roots

This weekend my husband and I sifted through fifteen years of papers and pictures we had stashed in boxes in our garage. We found college essays, old emails we'd sent to each other, and baby pictures of us that our parents had handed over years ago.

In among the pictures, I found one that captured five generations of the women in my family.

I remembered this picture. It used to make me laugh when I was a girl, because the older the generation, the shorter the woman. I was around eleven or twelve in the picture; I was the tallest female standing.

What I noticed this time, however, was not only the stair-step quality about that picture; I noticed the women—their strength, their poise, their certainty that life was theirs for the taking.

There was white-haired Memama, who lost her husband young; who lived, alone, in the house he built her until the day she fell on its sidewalk and died during hip surgery; who slept with a pistol under her pillow, just in case. She was legendary in our family. She lived until she was one hundred years and two weeks old.

There was her daughter, my Nana, who had false teeth and a pacemaker, who wouldn't go anywhere without her orange-tinted lipstick, who made the best chicken and dumplings in the South. She lost a son early, in a car accident, practically raised his kids, lost her husband in his garden, and drove way too fast, as though daring life to take her, too. She would have loved to know the Astros won the World Series this year. She lived until she was ninety.

There was her daughter, my Memaw, who had a fiery temper (especially on roadways), loved the color purple, and stayed up late snacking on Riesen caramels, potato chips, and Werther's original hard candies. She was opinionated (just ask my Uncle John), bitter at the edges, and one of the most generous people I've ever known. She lived without her husband for more than thirty years, in a house all by herself, until she died at seventy-four.

And there is my mom, who spent years raising her three kids as a single mom before my stepdad came along. She made hard choices, worked more than one job, and sacrificed her dream of becoming a geologist to become a school librarian (which I think she liked better anyway). Today she runs the Jackson County Library I grew up visiting and stocks every book I write.

Sometimes I forget this long line of strong women who stand behind me. I forget that they are in my bones, in my veins, in my mind and heart. I forget that their strength is also my strength, that the greatness that lived in them is also the greatness living in me.

Looking at this picture makes me wish that the three women in it who are no longer living were here—to walk, unafraid, out the doors of her old house on the wrong side of the tracks; to yell raucously for the Astros and remind us that she'd been rooting for the right team all along; to laugh until the sound shakes itself out. To meet my sons, to show them what strong women look like, to share a past that is wholly unimaginable to children today.

But the ones who remain—my mother, my aunt, my sister, and me—will tell their stories, live in their strength, and carry on.

We will remember.

60. Put Down the Phones

We've had the conversation before.

Many times before, actually.

When I'm talking, when I walk into a room, when my husband has just walked in the door from being gone for three hours, I don't want to compete with a phone.

I'm just reading an article, he says.

Well, I'm just trying to talk. But I shut my mouth.

You're mad, he says.

No, I say.

I'm trying to read something, he says. Why are you mad about that?

Maybe I *am* a little mad. But mostly disappointed.

I always feel like I'm interrupting, I say.

Just give me a minute, he says.

I give him twenty.

I will never be as interesting as a phone, and if someone even wants to make that comparison, they don't deserve to hear what comes out of my mouth.

Just before bed, he asks me what I wanted to say. I've already forgotten.

It doesn't matter, I say.

I really want to hear it, he says.

Really. I've forgotten, I say. Maybe I'll remember tomorrow. It probably wasn't that important.

And it probably wasn't.

Still. I want to look for the moments where I can put the phone down. The world exists outside of screens, and if we're not careful, we'll miss it.

61. When Words Hurt, Remember Who You Are

Words have power. I know this as a writer. I know it, too, as a vulnerable, thinking, feeling person.

Words have stilled my pen—words that confuse, condemn, scratch fear down the length of my back. How is it that I can be, one day, so sure and the next so shaken by words?

The words followed me home. *You write things that seem like you're relying on your own power. You exalt yourself. You don't have enough of the name of Jesus in your writing.*

For a week I can't write at all, the voices of my evangelical past rising from the oceans in which I cast them long ago when I was given a vision so sharp, so clear, I realized I didn't need the approval—or understanding—of people anymore. I had a purpose, a plan, a talent that would be poured out on a world full of people in need of remembering who they are: significant, worthy, beloved.

All week I thought instead. I thought of all the people over the years who have tried to tell me who I need to be—some of them because I'm a woman, and in the evangelical church tradition in which I grew up that means I do not have authority to exercise my voice if it means I am placed in leadership over a man; some of them because I came from the wrong side of the tracks, so to speak; some of them merely because some enjoy presuming to know more about another's life than the life-liver does.

I thought and thought and thought—about the man who said I'd never be a poet because he hated any poem that mentioned religion (or so I'd presumed my sophomore year of college; my ego could not construct another explanation at the time); the best friend who betrayed me and later told me it was because she didn't want people to think I was perfect, oh, and also I was marrying the wrong person (I've been married to the "wrong" person for fifteen years and counting); the college advisor who told me I should choose a major besides "English with an emphasis on creative writing and Shakespeare studies" because what were the odds I'd find a viable job with a specialty like that and how many writers actually made a living off their writing—but hey, journalists did!; the pastor who told my husband he could not serve as a worship pastor at his church if I were a singer on the team because his church was the big leagues and I didn't make the cut.

People have been trying to tell me what I'm supposed to do with my life for most of my life. Be a journalist—you have the writing chops. Serve the children's ministry—you certainly have enough children. Speak more of Jesus's name in your writing—it's your purpose and mandate, right here in this Bible you claim to follow.

What people who presume to know what I am supposed to do with my life and my work and my family and my self always seem to forget about me is that I have never operated out of a deficiency of vision or purpose. I have known, for a very long time, what I am supposed to do and how I am supposed to do it. I don't always get it right, of course, because I am not perfect, but I do always try to err on the side of love, least harm, most *tikkun olam*—the restoration of what has been broken.

We don't all have the same vision, the same purpose; we are very different people, all of us needed in our different ways. We share some edges of purpose—to love, to shine light and hope into darkness and despair, to leave the world better and more just than it was before—but the specifics of our purpose are as different as we are. It would be a boring world, I think, if that were not true. As I use my pointed poetry to illuminate injustice, so another uses an allegorical story to address discrimination. As one uses dance to remind an audience there is beauty in the world, so another uses documentary photography. As one uses melody to sing a song of love, so another uses art to flood the senses with truth, which leads to understanding, which leads to worth and significance. Who can say that one is better than the other?

Some will, in fact, say one is better than the other.

I lost a week of writing because I am only human, because though I try to convince myself that I don't care what other people think, that I only care about my mission and purpose, which I believe was given to me by God but which others might dismiss as anything but, I always find, at times like this, that I *do* care. But I also know that what comes between me and my vision and purpose—to love others as wholly as I can, to remind them who they are, to restore what has been broken in the hearts and lives of real, breathing people—deserves no place of power in my field of vision.

So I cast it away.

Tonight, for the first time in seven days—longer than I think I have ever gone without writing—I pick up my pen, the scratching sounds filling my silent bedroom like a sudden rush of water.

Beside me, I see the ghost of a smile graze the corners of my husband's lips.

62. Keep an Open Heart and Mind

Another shooting happened, less than three hundred miles from me. Ten dead, ten more injured, another school put on lockdown.

I want to live in a world where I don't have to worry about sending my kids to school because they might not come back home. I want to live in a world where kids who might be potential shooters are identified and helped, rather than further isolated by suspension sentences and restraining orders. I want to live in a world where we see all people—victims and shooters—with dignity and worth and honor and love.

We are not there yet.

At moments like these, my thoughts always turn toward the families of victims. But they don't ever stop there. They turn, also, to the families of the shooters, toward the shooters themselves. What kind of pain must they be dealing with to feel that this was the only solution to their problems? What kind of sorrow must be present in the mother who raised a shooter? What can we do?

There are, of course, many issues. And we all like simple solutions, but these things have no simple solutions. We must be willing to ask more questions, look at more angles, have open-ended conversations. We must put ourselves in the shoes of all involved—victims, bystanders, shooters—and practice radical empathy to examine the hard questions. We must trade our pointing fingers for open hands.

Understanding and love are some of the most powerful ingredients for changing the world.

63. Be a Peacemaker

In the past few weeks I've found myself backing away from social media, disengaging from the dividing lines that seem to mark us as a contemporary society, shielding myself from the angry news, the dehumanizing words, the conversations that feature more talkers than listeners.

I am, by nature, a peacemaker. I don't like to step inside conflict, to shake up waters that I'd rather remain tranquil and still. And sometimes that means I haven't spoken when I really needed to speak, when I felt the words damming up inside, when I noticed that someone was bulldozing another's identity.

Identity is a shaky thing in the first place; we're often not entirely sure we've really found it. We uncover it, we bury it, we uncover it again. We don't always live into it perfectly.

When our identity is further shaken for the purpose of corroborating right or wrong in an argument that will prove ridiculous in the grand scheme of things, I balk. Not always publicly, but always privately.

I know what I'm supposed to speak; the words come easily for me. But sometimes I'm too tired to be brave. And, besides, what about peace?

I've spent quite a bit of time recently thinking about what it means to be a peacemaker. Thinking about how we preserve dignity and honor in the face of ever-present conflict. Thinking about my own convictions and where they line up with peacemaking.

Sometimes the best way to understand something is to think about what it doesn't mean.

Peacemaking doesn't mean compromising on my values. It doesn't mean leaving behind my ideals. It doesn't mean pressing pause on my mission, which can be summed up by e.e. cummings's wise words: "love is the whole and more than all."

It doesn't always mean remaining silent.

The other day my husband stood at his computer, scrolling through Facebook, though I've told him it's not a good time to be on Facebook and we have better things to do and create. He saw a post from a friend that shocked and disappointed him. He said, "How do I keep from spending all my time on social media, helping people look at facts instead of opinions?" He was asking, because he wanted to set this friend straight, to present the factual details that could be used to create a more informed opinion—regardless of whether or not that opinion actually changed.

It's a difficult question to answer, and the answer will be different for everyone, at different times. Some weeks I know I have better things on which to train my focus; some weeks I feel compelled to impress knowledge and compassion onto and into hearts. Sometimes my peacemaking looks like remaining silent; sometimes it looks like bringing a sword (metaphorically speaking, of course).

Sometimes the peacemakers are the people who speak most boldly (in love, remember), let that truth unfold in the hearts of hurting people, and usher in peace that is large and expansive enough to overcome fear and hate and dividing lines. Sometimes our very presence is peace: We show people they are not alone, that they can endure, that we are all the same, deep down. Sometimes we become peacemakers in the things we create.

And we must not neglect to do what is necessary for ourselves, to remain at peace. We cannot be peacemakers if we are not ourselves at peace. For me, that looks like scheduling a time of meditation every morning. It looks like taking frequent Sabbaticals from social media. It looks like culling acquaintances from my friends list. It looks like spending time with the people I love, in person, here, now.

In becoming peacemakers, we must have standards: We cannot compromise who we are, for what we stand, and what we know of love—that it forever endures, no matter what.

That is as true for us as it is for "them."

64. Find a Way to Give the World Yourself

I was walking my sons to school the other day when the woman crossing children at the crosswalk said, "I looked up your book yesterday."

I never know what to say in situations like these, so I just said, "Oh, yeah?"

She said, "Yeah." She didn't say anything else about my book (I can't say I wasn't glad). She moved on to tell me that she's been urging her husband to write a book for a while. She said, "I think he would write it well, but he just doesn't have the time."

I can empathize with this completely. My first traditionally published book was written in short bursts—half an hour here, fifteen minutes there. Time—or the lack thereof—is one of the largest reasons more people don't write.

But having found the time, I know, too, that there is another, larger reason that more people don't ever finish their book, and it's this: Writing demands much of authors.

That "much" includes, of course, time, but even more than that it includes everything a writer gives. What I mean by that is both simple and complicated: A writer gives herself.

There is not a book I have written yet that does not contain large pieces of me. I split open my heart and my soul and my brain and meet the page in the most vulnerable place, disrobing family secrets (even if they are hidden behind fiction or metaphor), examining the darkest places of my mind, telling stories I might rather forget. There are projects that have nearly broken me—a current one is a memoir I'm working on about the first summer I went to see my dad and his new family after my parents divorced. It took me three years to write down a fictional story about a suicidal teenager because within the story are pieces of myself, my teenage years with my brother, and a current ongoing struggle with my pre-teen son. I cried through the final draft of a picture book that just went out on submission—because it contains so much raw, unbridled pain and extravagant hope.

Writing a book is not as simple as choosing an idea, doing research, carving out the time to put words on a page. Writers give themselves, too.

This is partially why, when an author's book finally releases into the world, they feel so much elation mixed up with fear and unease. We are known more fully by our work. And we know that not everyone will be kind to those pieces of us out in the world, threading into our stories or essays or poems. We hope they will be, but we don't live in an ideal world, and the words of others sometimes sting in our most vulnerable places.

Before I get started on a new project, I always take a deep breath, close my eyes, and repeat to myself these words from Maya Angelou:

"My wish is that you continue. Continue to be who you are, to astonish a mean world with your acts of kindness."

Though I know it will be difficult to peel off those scabs that have grown over verbal abuse and use the old wounds to tell a story about the pain and confusion of a boy, I know I must—because other children live in a situation exactly like that, and they need to know they are worthy of acceptance and a future and the greatest of love. I enter into the ache, I let it blast through my chest, and I give all of myself to the storytelling, to the examination of difficult things, to the redemption of what has been broken. *Tikkun olam.*

I give because I love my readers. I give because I desire to see a world in which every person realizes their worth and significance. I give because it is my purpose, because it is the way in which I meet people and leave a part of myself with them. Because I take seriously the words of Fred Rogers: "If you could only sense how important you are to the lives of those you meet; how important you can be to the people you may never even dream of. There is something of yourself that you leave at every meeting with another person."

I hope I never hold back.

65. Don't Forget the Vulnerable

I recently had the privilege and pleasure of returning to the library I visited every Saturday as a kid. My mom is the library director there, and she asked me to do an author event. I readily agreed. With a crowd of old school friends, old teachers, and strangers, I talked about my journey from small-town girl to published author.

I came from humble beginnings, but I always knew I wanted to be an author. I soon learned that people like me—the poor—weren't supposed to be authors; we were supposed to be workers, not creators. We were supposed to try harder to pull ourselves from the cycle of poverty, and creative work wasn't *real* work. We were supposed to accept our lot in life and go about our business if not happily, then at least diligently.

Though she didn't divorce my father until I was eleven, my mom spent most of my childhood as a single mom, while my father was out of state working a job that didn't provide her much money, if any at all. Money was tight. She was creative and stretched it as far as she could. She worked two jobs—sometimes three—to do it. But she always seemed able to provide me with an endless supply of stapled-together white paper and sharpened pencils. I ran through these blank "books" rapidly, writing and illustrating stories very similar to *Little House on the Prairie*, (though the drawings were nowhere near the quality of Garth Williams's illustrations).

In middle school my English and Reading teachers recognized something in me. They told me I was good at writing, and that made me think maybe I could do it. In high school my teachers affirmed that gift, inviting me to enter writing competitions, participate in literary criticism to hone my writer's eye, publish in small magazines, and develop my skill in big and small ways. I got a full scholarship to college for not just my GPA and valedictorian status, but, I believe, the strength of my entrance essay, which my high school counselor encouraged me to write.

I speak out often on behalf of the poor—about their need for support, the complicated circumstances that keep them stranded in lack, the way we are all different even while we share the same seams of a story. And any time I speak about it, old high school friends come out to say, "Yes, but you made it out. Why can't they?"

I made it out; why can't they?

It's a difficult question to answer, and, of course, there are never simple answers to any questions. I made it out because I hailed from different circumstances—I had a mother who believed in me and told me every chance she got. I made it out because I had the right personality; I've always been tenacious, even while carrying a good measure of self-doubt, and that helped me climb from the pit (not without a few falls, but I've never been one to stay down for long). I made it out because all along my way I had someone calling me higher—people who loved me and wanted the best for me and believed I could actually accomplish it.

My making it out was a group effort; I am not who I am—did not become who I am—alone. I am who I am because of the people in my life.

Every situation is different, which means I can't say for certain why someone can't climb out of their own poverty pit. Poverty is a cycle for a reason; many don't have the support or fortune to pull themselves up by the bootstraps, as the saying goes. Many don't have bootstraps at all; they fell off a long time ago.

I often tell people that I feel as though I was swept along in a tide that I could not control and could not stop, as if there was something invisible carrying me to where I am now. For me, that tide is God; for others it is, perhaps, a coincidence. A lucky streak. A fortunate turn of events. I am not here to argue semantics; I only know that I have become because of a long line of people believing in, supporting, and encouraging me to become.

And today, as any other day, I feel incredibly grateful that I never walked alone. And I think, as I so often do, about those who are alone. I hope we can find them and give them what my helpers gave me: hope, identity, and a way out.

66. Read and Re-read as Many Books as You Can

Recently I talked with a group of third- and fifth-graders about how to cultivate creativity in a young life, and one of the first questions they asked me was this one: Who were your biggest influences when you were a kid?

I hadn't pre-prepared for any of the questions they asked me, even though I should have known they would come. Kids are curious about what (and who) shapes adults to become who they are. And there were so many influences along my journey—teachers and my mom, of course, but mostly authors.

Even as a child, I was a reader. A writer. A girl who knew what I wanted to be before I ever had a clue what it meant to grow up.

During a recent year of writing poetry based off the words of famous writers, artists, and influential people, I stumbled across this quote from Francois Mauriac, a French novelist, dramatist, critic, poet, and journalist: "Tell me what you read and I'll tell you who you are is true enough, but I'd know better if you told me what you re-read."

These words ring true in my life.

There are so many good things to read. I read mostly middle grade fiction, more young adult fiction recently. I read a poem a day from various poets—especially favorites like W.H. Auden, Mary Oliver, William Carlos Williams. I read some adult literature, but not much. I read the classics.

What I re-read is a much smaller list, but it points to who I am. The most re-read book on my shelf is Charles Dickens' *A Christmas Carol*, followed closely by Emily Bronte's *Wuthering Heights*, Madeleine L'Engle's *A Wrinkle in Time*, Louisa May Alcott's *Little Women*, Rilke's collected poetry, Scott O'Dell's *Island of the Blue Dolphins*, Ray Bradbury's *Fahrenheit 451* and *Something Wicked This Way Comes*, everything Maya Angelou and Toni Morrison have written, and Katherine Applegate's *Home of the Brave* and *The One and Only Ivan*.

Though we rarely recognize it, books shape us into who we are. We spend hours, days, sometimes even weeks with them, and we are always changed by the end of them. And the ones we re-read change us even more.

Books offer us new ideas, whisper who we might become, open us to the lives of other people who are different than we are.

They show us a way forward. They prove that we can overcome, we can do better, we are made to be heroes of whatever story we're living. They remind us that this—the shadow we're wrestling with right now—is not the end of the story.

Isn't it wonderful to feel seen, heard, loved?

67. Teach the Next Generation What Matters

Today I had a frank conversation with my young sons about civil rights—or, more specifically, women's rights.

It began like this: My oldest son said, "If women did not have the right to work, vote, and contribute to society, would that mean you couldn't write your stories?"

"Well, there's a possibility that my voice would be silenced in a world like that," I said. I hesitated before continuing. "And, in fact, it wasn't so long ago that women did not have a right to work or vote or contribute to society in any way beyond their homes."

My sons looked at each other, eyes wide with horror.

"That would be really bad," the ten-year-old said.

"I wouldn't want to live in that world," the eight-year-old said.

Indeed. And so onward we press, always looking toward progress, innovation and a more just world where all men *and women* are created equal.

68. Don't Let the World Make You Small

It is difficult being a strong woman.

To have our opinions, which are not always the "right and proper" opinions, to assert these opinions, to be dismissed for them; to be passionate about the things we are passionate about; to step out into the wilderness that holds no shred of similarity to the popular way of things embraced by the "in" group—it is not without its dangers.

There are days my insides have burned liquid from the passion of my purpose, and there are days my insides have frozen solid because I don't know if I should say what needs to be said—I have watched too many strong women get knocked to their knees, and I don't know if I have what it takes to get back on my feet when the same comes for me.

Strong women brave the consequences of their strength. There is never a shortage of critics and judgment and misunderstanding leveled at strong women, because women, historically, have been shoved into neat and pretty—convenient—boxes. Stay here, stay silent, stay small.

The problem is that I have never liked boxes, the way they press in on all sides and make it hard to breathe, the way they cut off the light with a darkness that feels inescapable, the way they smell of dust and fear and the death of what had lived. So though I know what a strong will and heart and mind can do to a woman's reputation, I choose to step out of the box, tape it up, and toss it back at the ones who would like me to remain curled up inside it, silent and small.

    I will not be silent. I will not be small.

69. Don't Apologize for Who You Are

I'm sorry for being a girl.

I'm sorry for stating my opinion, which is different than yours.

I'm sorry for taking up space, overflowing from the box you'd like me to fold up in.

I'm sorry for having dreams and believing I might be able to achieve them.

I'm sorry for expecting a fair wage even though you clearly work harder than I do, judging by the sweat.

I'm sorry for carrying a few extra pounds, instead of fitting your ideal image of what a woman is supposed to look like.

I'm sorry I forgot to shave my legs and now you have to stare at hair you don't think should be there.

I'm sorry for not dressing like a woman and feeling more comfortable in my workout pants, instead of a tight miniskirt and heels.

I'm sorry for not being good at the domestic side of the equation, instead of playing the part of supermom, super partner, super homemaker, super worker (for less pay).

I'm sorry for being so sensitive and not shaking it off.

I'm sorry for crying instead of growing a thick skin.

I'm sorry for valuing my body enough to say no, you may not pinch, poke, or touch it without my permission.

I'm sorry for believing I could be somebody.

I'm sorry for being loud and speaking up where you think I should stay quiet.

I'm sorry for disagreeing with you instead of playing the part of mindless puppet: *You're right. I didn't think about that. Thank you for explaining it so succinctly.*

I'm sorry for rattling chains, instead of remaining a quiet prisoner in a man's world.

I'm sorry for being intelligent and intellectually challenging.

I'm sorry for being a woman.

The truth is, I'm not sorry for any of it.

70. Hold Fast to Your Purpose

The other day my husband and I were finishing dinner for our sons, and I, having come off a high from my current work in progress, which finally hit its sweet spot after two weeks of struggling, said, "I don't know if I've said this recently, but I really, really love what I do."

My husband hears this often; I can't help but express gratitude for the gift of doing what I love—creating what was not there before. I love the entire process—researching, brainstorming, drafting, revising, editing. It feels like a sacred process to me, where truth is mixed purposefully with fiction, reality merges with story, hopes and dreams and affirmations of identity crawl into carefully chosen words. It is, I believe, a great privilege to remind people who they are, to reassure them they are loved, to tell them they are not alone, we belong to each other, we can do hard things, there is hope.

I find exquisite joy and wonder and satisfaction in this act of creation. But that joy and wonder and satisfaction gets challenged when I accidentally consider one tiny little piece of the process: numbers and reviews.

At times in my writer journey, I have created something and put it out there for the world to see, and the numbers have disappointed—there aren't enough likes, shares, hearts, comments, sales, whatever. Social media and the easy access of the Internet often make it difficult for a writer to create without looking at the numbers, and those numbers, at least for me, are like misty clouds fogging up my joy.

Reviews are another beast entirely. My agent, who also wrote and published a book last year, recently shared a twitter thread about how one reviewer of her book kept persistently tagging her in a negative review of the book. The reviewer tagged her multiple times, almost as though she wanted to make sure my agent saw just how much her book was hated.

That's enough to sometimes make a writer hold all her words close and forget about sharing them with the world. I often wonder if reviewers forget that a writer is a real person, a person who puts pieces of herself into her work, a person who works for months—sometimes years—to finish a project, a person who is full of insecurities and doubts and their own Voices of Doom that stem from their past and trauma and even, perhaps, already-noted reviews.

At the beginning of January, when I returned to work after two weeks of holiday with my family, I picked up a brand-new project and I slogged through the writing of it that whole first and second week. Plaguing me was a review I'd read of my first traditionally published book, *The Colors of the Rain*. It circled through my head and sat near the back of my eyes so every time I closed them, which I do to visualize scenes, those negative words flashed neon bright. The reviewer, an adult, had called my book unbelievable, had said she couldn't finish it. It didn't matter that the same day she posted this review a fifteen-year-old boy had thanked me for writing the book because it looked so much like his life and he felt seen and understood and like his experiences mattered. My book validated his life, reminded him that he was worth something greater than what he'd been through.

So after the first two weeks of slogging, I sat down and had a talk with myself. I said, *Remember your true audience. They need your book.*

And then I got to work.

Not everyone will love what I create. That's okay. The important thing is that I remember for whom I'm creating and why, and I leave the rest behind.

Lives can't be changed by contributions that don't exist.

71. Always Ask for What You Need

He said, "For someone who knows so clearly what you want, it's annoying to me—someone who doesn't have as clear an idea—that you have a hard time asking for it."

Maybe I'm too careful. Maybe there are times I need to step out of my accommodating, forgiving nature and assert myself.

"What's the worst that can happen?" he says.

I've never liked answering that question.

•

Being the owner of an overactive imagination, there are plenty of worst things that can happen. They all come creeping in at the slightest invitation—like the question, "What's the worst that can happen?"

I don't want to look any one of them in the eye, lest I lose my nerve.

•

I've typed the email a dozen times, and it still doesn't feel right. Have I really asked for what I want, or is it just another soft, kind, accommodating note that doesn't really say much?

I send it off to a writer friend.

She sends it right back with confirmation: It's just another soft, kind, accommodating note that doesn't really say much.

•

My sons are young, and my husband and I have tried to raise them in an environment that values good communication skills.

"Use your words" is something we say often when they feel upset or angry or sad. They are learning in ways their father and I—a generation that was taught to hide more than it revealed, to suck it up, get over it, life's got a lot of hard knocks, kid, take what's handed out without complaining—never did.

Maybe in their future, they will be able to use their words to ask for what they want.

Maybe they will be better than I have been.

•

I'm standing at my computer again. I sort through the questions: What do I want? What do I expect? What is the problem that keeps me from getting what I want or expect?

It all makes sense in my head, but when I get ready to write it down, my fingers feel stiff and uncooperative.

But I flex them, and the words, clunky and patchy at first, spill, stain, solidify.

•

We ask for what we want, because if we don't, the person on the other side of our asking won't know what we want. We ask to clarify, to make aware, to say that my needs and goals and desires are important, too, and we should work together to make sure we're both happy and reaching our full potential and doing what must be done.

We ask because we are important enough, too, to have our needs and goals and desires met.

•

I'm a woman. I've been told my whole life, in one way or another, that I shouldn't have needs or goals or desires. I've been tricked into believing, by immersion in a patriarchal society and faith or simply by an encounter with another individual, that my needs are not as important as others' needs. I've been shamed for my aspirations, my expectations, my dreams.

It's not an easy legacy to discard.

•

I send the email this time. Who knows if it will make a difference or if anything will change, but at least I know I've tried. At least I know that the next time I must ask for what I need I will be marginally better at it. At least I know I have said what needs saying, bared a small piece of myself, moved toward becoming something more than a passive spectator to my life and career.

And the whisper grows, if only by a hair: *I matter, too.*

72. Find Your Corner

This week I got a message from a friend telling me about an organization he was starting. This organization will find the fatherless children in his small city and pair them with male volunteers who can become like honorary fathers to them.

I thought this was a brilliant idea. I grew up fatherless, and I know what growing up fatherless can do to a child.

I immediately wanted to start my own organization in my city.

How many kids need that here? I thought. *A whole lot.*

The problem is that I have a purpose. A purpose that demands time and energy. A purpose just as important as that one.

As much as I want to do it all—because there are so many people in our world who need help—I can't. I am limited by time, energy, and resources, and if I try to spread what time, energy, and resources I have between all of the problems of the world, I will be inefficient at addressing even one of them.

This is where corners come in.

A boy I once dated used to enjoy watching boxing. If you've ever seen a boxing match, you know that when a round finishes, boxers retreat to a corner. This is their corner where they plan their next course of action, where they analyze their previous strategy, where they regroup and prepare to go back out into the ring and win the match.

Corners are the same for us.

We all have our corners of the world—the places where we can do the most good. There are a lot of corners in the world, though, and sometimes we get caught up in wanting to defend them all. We can't. It's simply not possible. There are too many needs in the world to personally address them all, and if we try, we will find ourselves unable to address even the one that presses the hardest on our heart.

We have to find our corners, and—here's the real challenge—we have to draw our boundary lines around them. The worst thing we can do for our corner is add another corner and then another and then another—until we have a whole room that splinters us into ineffective pieces.

There are times when I have spoken out about my corner of the world. And, inevitably, acquaintances will question my passion. They will say, "If you care so much about *that*, why don't you care about *this*?" It's not that I don't care about *this*. I care about a great many things. It's just that I know my corner. And in order to become the greatest force of change I can possibly be, I have to stay in that corner. I have to trust that others will step up and into that other corner.

So how do we find our corners?

I believe that process is unique to every person. But I also believe that we can start with our passions, our experiences, and our expertise. Often, where those things collide, we will find ourselves in the corner where we can make the most difference.

And that's how we change a piece of the world.

STRUGGLE

73. Remember That Life Goes On

Tonight, over dinner, I had to talk to my sons about cancer.

It's been pressing on my mind all day—the text from my sister-in-law. A week ago my brother, who never goes to doctors, went to a doctor. He woke up with a black veil over his left eye. He was nauseated to the point of disability. When he tried to walk, the world tilted, spun, and lost its sense of order.

They found a tumor.

It's cancer.

Brain cancer.

In less than a week he'll have brain surgery and begin chemotherapy. Everything is uncertain.

He could die, my eight-year-old said. Yes. He could.

He'll be sick, won't he, my seven-year-old said. Yes. He will.

Will it damage his brain? my ten-year-old asked. Maybe. We hope not.

What if they don't get it all?

Will it spread?

Will it happen to me?

So many of their questions I could not answer. It's cancer. It's unpredictable. It has no pattern, no measurable origin, no certain outcome.

Our dinner ended very quietly, like a reverent prayer. And fifteen minutes later, when they had all done their after-dinner chores without a single complaint, they were blissfully screeching on the trampoline out back.

I closed my eyes and listened to how predictably life goes on.

74. Examining the Deeper Things of Life is Valuable

The photos were alarming.

My mother, a librarian, had signed up for a deep tissue massage and ended up with two arms full of bruises. During the session, she'd voiced her discomfort. Was it supposed to be this painful? The masseuse told her that deep tissue massages are different than regular massages; they got down to the deeper knots and ironed them out.

And perhaps that's true; I don't know much about massage beyond the fact that I once dated a guy who was a masseuse (I was probably the most relaxed I'd ever been during the few months we dated).

My mother's massage had gone wrong—one had only to look at her blue-and-purple arms to see that.

For the last several years I have been working on a memoir about the first summer I visited my father and new stepmother and half-siblings after my parents' divorce. I have written and rewritten this story, over and over again, never completely satisfied and never, honestly, sure I want to go on. It is not an easy story. Those memories are not exactly comfortable to examine or even sit with for an extended period of time.

But writing is often like that deep tissue massage—the good kind. Of course we can go too far—press too deeply before we're ready—but if we are careful, writing, whether it's fiction, nonfiction, or poetry, can be like a gentle yet deep massage. Writing helps me come to terms with my past and the way it has shaped my present (and sometimes this piece alone is undeniably enlightening), and clarifies, too, what I will carry into my future. It may seem trite to some, but writing is, for me, a prayer—a prayer for healing, a prayer for *tikkun olam* (repairing what has been broken), a prayer of hope and love for the ones who read my work.

Because of this, I don't ever deny myself access to difficult memories. I write essays about what terrifies me, humiliates me, pains me. Sometimes I have to wait months or even years to set that story down on paper, and sometimes the words will go no farther than my current writing journal, but the act of writing alone—my prayer—is the deep tissue massage I need to come to terms with, accept, and even flourish in spite of whatever has happened.

It's been proven, time and time again, that writing is a therapeutic process. It mends painful memories, reduces stress, even helps pull the struggling out of depression (science proves this, but I have seen circumstantial evidence of it in my own life). It rids the body of toxins—as long as you don't press too hard or get stuck in the wrong places.

In my writing, my prayers, my deep tissue massage, I can rewrite my past into something hopeful; something that proves I was never a victim, I was always loved, held, and worthy; something that can tell my readers the same.

I don't know what I'll do with that memoir I've been writing and rewriting. It will likely end up as a fiction story, since I'm not entirely sure I want it out in the world as nonfiction. But regardless of what happens from here, the simple act of writing it has already done its deep work.

It has written over the painful past in giant permanent-marker letters: redeemed.

75. You Are Not Your Body

The body is an alien.

I can divorce myself from it, look at it objectively in the mirror as though it belongs to someone else. I can tell myself that it looks better than it does, and by the same token I can tell myself that it looks much worse. I don't know which viewpoint is the right one, honestly; my eyes trick me sometimes. My husband tells me my body is beautiful, but how do you believe a thing like that when your eyes tell you something different? Do you trust what he says? Do you trust what you see?

I want to love my body. I can't do it. I don't know why.

•

The body is a burden.

The other day we packed up in the car for a quick trip to Target (with kids in tow, it's never quick), and I casually mentioned that it would be nice to have a tummy tuck, get rid of this baby pooch my body got used to wearing in the eight years I wore pregnancy and postpartum like a familiar blanket. My husband gave me a dirty look and asked what the point of *that* would be—so that others would be impressed? I don't think it's about others, I said; I think it's about me, and sometimes (more often than he'd probably like to know), I think I would be so much happier if I could just get rid of this stomach once and for all. It's a shallow thing, I know. I'm not proud of it. In fact, I beat myself up about it, but we all carry around our mental and emotional scars and saddles, don't we? This one's mine.

I want to love my body. Most days that feels impossible. I don't know why.

•

The body is a blight.

I saw a woman at the pool yesterday, flawless body, smooth stomach, pretty curves in all the right places, and I imagined my husband looking at her for longer than was necessary. But I know he wasn't. I *know* he wasn't. I know that he loves me, wants to be with me, thinks I'm beautiful exactly as I am. But she was perfect, and I am not, not after six kids and the havoc that wreaks on a body. But six healthy kids—that's something, isn't it?

I want to love my body. I'm trying.

76. Life Will Usually Get Better If We Hold On

The maroon Honda Pilot was ambling through the school zones, keeping to the speed limit while other cars zoomed around it, oblivious to flashing yellow lights, or perhaps simply in too much a hurry to heed. I followed the rule-keeper, because I'm a rule-keeper myself.

This car was going slightly slower than the speed limit, but I was on my way back from a doctor's appointment and had nowhere important to be. The car provides a good thinking space, quiet, confined, automatic. So I remained behind the Pilot not only because of my non-hurry but also because I'd noticed a purple Crayola marker sitting on the lip of the Pilot's bumper. I wanted to see how long that purple marker would hang on through the starts and stops of traffic. I wanted to see it roll off the bumper and into the street, where it would likely embark on another journey, settling against the curb of the street or, less happily, smashed beneath the tires of another car.

But that purple marker held on, until the Pilot turned left on Knights Cross, where it disappeared from my view. It had held on for two miles—maybe more.

Dear Self:

Hold on like the purple marker.

77. Take Your Sick Days

A couple of weeks ago, I came down with the flu. I don't usually get a flu shot, but this year my husband kept reading about some terrible cases of the flu—cases where people died—and announced one Friday (with a clap!) that we were having a family outing: We were heading down to the local grocery store to get our flu shots.

Two days later I wound up with the flu.

My husband assures me there is no connection between the flu shot and the flu; I just want to point out that only two days passed between getting the shot and getting the flu.

I felt it coming on the first night, but I'm tough (or that's what I tell myself, at least), so the next morning, when I wanted to stay in bed, I gave myself a silent pep talk, so as not to wake my sleeping husband, and climbed out of bed anyway.

Fortunately, it happened to be my turn to work in the morning, which meant my husband was in charge of the childcare (we trade off our days—sometimes I take care of our sons in the morning and work in the afternoon, sometimes he takes care of our sons in the morning and works in the afternoon. One of us is always working a morning or afternoon shift while the other is always on childcare for the morning or afternoon. It's a great arrangement that works for us—but certainly not for everyone.).

As I stood at my computer, trying to write, my head kept

getting heavier and heavier. So I sat down to work. When my head felt even too heavy to hold up while sitting down, I climbed into bed.

That's where my husband found me, two hours later, when he brought me some tea.

Sick days are not easy to negotiate when you're a parent. There are always children to redirect, always dinner to get on the table, always bedtime.

Always, always bedtime.

My body burned up with fever, couldn't hold itself up, and rejected every attempt I made to climb from my bed and see to my family.

But we had to quarantine anyway, so no one else would get it. Which meant I had to stay in my room, shut away from everyone. In bed. Sleeping. Resting. Doing absolutely nothing for the three days it took me to get well.

No one else got it.

I slept hard, those three days, and when I was done being sick (it was actually a couple of weeks before I felt fully recovered), I felt refreshed and more than ready to get back to work.

Sometimes being sick provides the perfect opportunity to take a step back, slow things down, and rest.

78. Hindsight Can Sometimes Be Foresight

He took out his video camera, and I did the same thing I always do: I turned away.

It happens every time a camera comes out—still camera or video camera, it makes no difference.

A friend came this week to do some documentary pictures of me and my family, and I loved it when she turned the camera on my children but felt somewhat uncomfortable when she turned them on me.

Those pictures are forever.

I wished I could have lost a little more weight.

I just won't share the ones I don't like—meaning the ones that make me look other than I want to look (all of them that contain me in the frame?).

I have a complicated relationship with pictures—I hate them at the time they're taken, and then, when I look back on them, I compare my present self to that past. The past woman is always better, younger, thinner, more beautiful.

I live life in the rearview mirror.

I was so much thinner then.

I should have enjoyed it while it lasted.

Gosh, I looked so much younger.

I always think, *I wish I'd enjoyed that photo session more. Let them take more pictures of me.*

Because maybe Future Me will one day look back at Present

Me and say, *Wow. She really was beautiful.*

So before the photo shoot is over, I grin with my sons and enjoy the snapping of the camera.

Grateful we have this opportunity.

79. Believing in Yourself is Easier With a Team

I sat in my bed, reading. My eight-year-old appeared by the side of the bed and said, "The speech teacher took me out of class today. She said I say my 's' sound wrong."

I knew this already; I'd been in communication with his teacher about it. I said, "Oh yeah? How did it go?"

"She taught me how to do it right. But I forgot." He danced out of the room, as though the conversation was now done. I watched the doorway for a minute, thinking maybe he'd gone to get something.

A few minutes later, when I'd returned to my book, he crept back inside my room. "I don't know if I'll ever be able to say my 's' right," he said. Before I could answer, he shot from the room again, this time racing his words out.

It didn't take him long to return. He said, "It's something like this." He tried to say an "s." He tried again. And again. His eyes filled. "I can't do it."

I took him in my arms and told him that just because he couldn't say the "s" sound correctly doesn't mean there's anything wrong with him. I don't always know the right thing to say at times like these, but I do know that kids need reminding—often—that there is nothing wrong with them, they are brilliantly spectacular as is, they are loved. I always start there.

He pulled away and said, "What if I don't ever say them right?" He looked at the ground, not at me.

This son is my pessimist. He will try and try and try until he is weary from trying, but he will rarely believe, even in the trying, that anything good will come of it. When he loses something, it will surely be gone forever (but he'll still keep looking). When a friend isn't home to play with him for a day, he'll probably never be able to play with this friend again (but he'll still knock on the door and ask tomorrow). When he has to clean up his mess before tech time, he'll probably never, ever, ever be done (but it'll only take him a minute).

I could feel his anxiety, hanging like a heavy cloud between us.

I said, "How old are you?"

"Eight."

"For eight years you've been saying the 's' sound wrong. It will take more than one session with the speech teacher to correct your habit." I paused to make sure he was still listening. He was playing with something on my bed, his head tilted a little. I knew his ears were tuned to me. I said, "You'll get it. I believe in you."

Sometimes a parent believing is enough.

I've had to reassure him of this same thing several times over the last weeks. There's nothing wrong with you, remember who you are, you'll get it. With enough repetition, the words will get lodged so deeply in him that he'll never get them out.

In the middle of all that repeating, all that reminding, we continue to help him practice his "s" sound, perfect it, have a little fun with it. And maybe, by the end of all this, when the "s" sound comes easily and naturally as though it were never a problem in the first place, he'll realize that nothing is impossible when you have a team.

80. Interruptions Can Be Magical

I was alone in my bedroom. It was Friday night, the time when my husband and I schedule our weekly at-home date night. He picks up takeout and we spread out a blanket on our bed and watch some Netflix while we eat. He was already on his way to pick up a chicken sandwich we'd share, along with some chips and queso. My sons were in the next room, reading. I usually take the time alone to write a little.

This particular night I was in the middle of what I think was a profound thought—and the door flew open. My three-year-old burst through it, smiling at me, effectively ejecting me from my profound thought and planting me right back in the real world.

"I want to have you," he said.

I felt a little annoyed, but I smiled and patted the spot next to me on the bed. He climbed up and showed me the Stitch stuffed animal (from *Lilo and Stitch*) he had brought with him. Stitch is attached to a slap bracelet that I'm surprised still works in this house of destructive boys.

My son bounded off the bed after a few minutes, climbed into the wing chair where I normally write, and used Stitch to turn off the light.

"Did you see that, Mama?" he said. "Stitch turned the light off with his tail!" His blue eyes sparkled with a delighted gleam, and I could see his tongue smashed between his teeth.

My writing was forgotten. I had to bask in his joy, his smile, his pleasure at having turned off the light with Stitch's tail.

He climbed back down from the chair, launched at me for a kiss, and scrambled toward the door.

"I love you," I said.

"I love you, too, Mama," he said as he bounded out of the room, Stitch flying in parabolas beside him.

Magic is everywhere.

I'm glad I had my eyes open to see it.

81. Accept That You Will Become Like Your Grandparents

My grandmother used to save newspaper articles and clippings from *Reader's Digest* (the large-print edition in later years) for the different people in her life. She'd hand me manila envelopes with cutouts paper-clipped together—about the lives of writers, the state of journalism, fitness for runners. She'd see something and investigate, or perhaps it was in the middle of reading that a family face would pop into her mind. Once she finished the piece, she would take the scissors and cut it out and store it away, until the next time she saw the person whose name she wrote on the tab in all capital letters.

I didn't much understand this urge of hers when I was younger. The articles she passed along to me in clasped envelopes or manila folders seemed like random bits and nothing more. Sometimes they came, unexpectedly, in the mail. Sometimes she underlined things, highlighted sentences, wrote something in the margins. Most of the time she left it alone, and I had to decode what she was trying to say.

The other day I was reading a short article in *National Geographic* (*National Geographic* is to me what *Reader's Digest* was to my grandmother) about a man who climbed a mountain without a rope. Free climbing, they call it. It's remarkably dangerous, which is why it's relatively rare. The writer reported about a man who had successfully completed the highest free climb anyone had ever attempted. While that part was interesting enough, it wasn't what made me think of my husband. What made me think of my husband was the fact that someone filmed a documentary about this man's climb.

My husband has a side job: documentary filmmaking. The article included information about the equipment used for the filming (which my husband will often talk about, though I can't usually follow), how the documentary filmmaker safely filmed the climb, and the number of hours required for preparation alone.

I dog-eared the page, thinking my husband would enjoy the article.

Later that night, when all the kids were finally in bed, I mentioned the article to my husband. He seemed lukewarm about it, much like I was back when my grandmother would hand me articles she'd saved for me. I handed it to him anyway, said, "I really think you'd enjoy it." He set the magazine on his bedside table. It'll take him months to read it—or maybe he'll read it tomorrow.

Either way, I could imagine my grandmother, who's been dead ten years, smiling, saying, "You see?"

And I do.

82. Recognize the Moments of Synchronicity

Tonight we walked along the road to the elementary school my sons attend. They wore brand-new superhero costumes that I'd spent too much money on—Kylo Ren, BB-8, Batman, Spider-Man, Hulk, and Captain America running, skiing, skipping, or hanging on my arm.

We were headed to the Scholastic book fair, and once inside the school library, I watched my sons wander around browsing the shelves like I used to do at my own Scholastic book fair. I remember feeling so excited to be there and more than ready to pick my very own book (probably from the two dollar stack). My sons picked up and put back books, the same excitement radiating from their faces.

And for a moment, the child self and the adult self were linked, a connection fostered by the shining light in my sons' eyes.

83. Let Children Break the Rules Every Now and Then

The other night I was passing through the hallway between our home library and my bedroom when I saw my youngest, who is two, running through his own hallway. His hair, which is on the long side, rippled behind him, and he was flapping his arms as he ran, laughing about how it felt to have wings.

I waved my husband to my side and whispered, "Look how adorable he is."

We'd already put him to bed, but there he was, darting back and forth, laughing hysterically, flapping his wings, unaware of his watchers. He looked like he might take off and fly.

Sometimes bedtime has to wait so a little boy can learn what it feels like to spread his wings and soar.

84. Look For the Activities that Remind You Who You Are

I've started running again.

It began with a handful of miles—three or four, then quickly escalated to the six I used to run in college, when I would get up every day at five a.m. and run the miles before 8 a.m. classes. My body remembers the routine; it's moved back into the ridges carved out over four years of my past.

The running gives me a sense of control. There's so much in my life that feels somewhat out of control, and it's comforting to have that segment of time—an hour, maybe more—when I have almost complete control—over my breath, the distance I run, the speed with which I run it. I belong to myself, and my mind stills, and it is only the steps, the breath, the path before me.

Running connects me fully to a moment, but it's not only that mysterious connection that calls to me on the days I don't schedule a run. It is the past, too.

For twelve years I have been a mother. I have given myself fully to my children. I have coaxed them through tantrums, taught them about emotions and how to read, aligned myself to their desires and needs so I can nurture and mold them into independent human beings who think and feel and decide for themselves. There is still a way to go; my oldest son is twelve, my youngest is four. They still need me, but not in quite the same way.

Two years ago, five years ago, it would have felt inconceivable to me that I would wake at five a.m. and spend an hour running six miles or more. Time to myself was short and tight. If I had an hour to myself, I would not spend it running.

But time has widened now. There are moments when I find myself alone in my home library, when my sons are playing happily in the backyard and I can open a book and read a page or two without interruption. There are moments I realize I've been staring into space, daydreaming for half an hour, and no one needed me. There are moments I can bookmark to run.

Maybe all this means I am losing part of myself—the part that was an ever-present, always-on-duty mother. My sons seek their father's advice for things now, not just mine. But maybe it also means that I am gaining back a long-lost part of myself, returning to a past me, remembering who I am, who I was—this person who looked forward to running six or more miles a day for the peace and quiet—the freedom—it gave her.

85. Schedule a Weekend Without Kids Every Now and Then

This weekend my parents took some sons and my in-laws took some sons, and my husband and I were alone, and it was a blissful two days spent staying up as late as we wanted and sleeping in as late as we could.

We:
went out to eat
got tattoos
test drove a minivan
finished our sentences without interruption
recorded a song
slept until 9 a.m.
watched a movie without the door swinging open
ate sweets without kids begging for a taste
I can't wait for the next one.

86. Nap Often

He asks me if I would like to take a nap with him, but I'm reading, I say. I rarely get a chance to read unless all of them are sleeping. Most of them are. But it's his eyes, the deep brown of them, that make me say, "Want to lie down with me?" after only a few minutes.

I slide my arm under his head, and he embraces me, snuggling closer. The top of his head smells of sweat and the outdoors. His heat radiates, swelling from his body so I have to kick off the bottom of the blanket encompassing us. His body thrums with his effort to keep still, and I know he'll only succeed for a handful of minutes. So I close my eyes and remember those first days after his birth, when he slept close to me, just like this, a tiny thing, warm, wrinkly, smelling brand new.

The clock ticks, and, in the end, he decides he's not tired after all. He's gone in a moment, his warmth still lining the blanket.

87. Enjoying Work Makes Time Fly

"Can I show you this real quick?"

My oldest son held out the old phone we gave him for his creative projects and a bit of structured technology time. I was putting the last touches on dinner—some baked chicken, some roasted beets and zucchini, and slices of watermelon for dessert. I was moments away from calling in the rest of my sons, from hearing them all complain about how gross dinner looked, from sitting down and trying to remain present.

I've had a lot on my mind lately. My first traditionally published book had just gone to press, I was waiting to hear back about a potential deal on a second one, and a third manuscript was not quite there yet, giving me fits and starts, making me wonder if it might not just be easier to give up on it.

This summer has felt like a constant battle to remain present.

So I watched the video, impressed by how meticulously my son arranged his LEGO mini figures and took their pictures and set the scene for a story.

"You put a lot of work into that," I said.

"Yeah," he said.

"How long did it take you?"

"An hour."

An hour for five seconds of captured stop motion video. He is more patient that I'd ever known him to be. And, like it always does when faced with a moment of brilliance from my children, my heart looked up, straightened from its wilting posture, squared its shoulders, and said, *Life is grand, isn't it?*

Until it was time to do after-dinner chores and the same son who spent an hour arranging tiny LEGO pieces and taking pictures and making a brilliant film could not be bothered to spend fifteen minutes rinsing and stacking dishes into the dishwasher.

The things we love are much easier to spend time doing than the things we loathe.

88. Children Are Only Ours For a Short Time

Yesterday my husband took my oldest son to his brand-new middle school. It was schedule-pickup day, when middle school students get their schedule and are then given the opportunity to walk through it and familiarize themselves with the rhythm and location of their classes. I wanted to go, but I didn't want to take all our other children, and I knew this was something my husband needed to do with our son. So I let him go—with this entreaty: Take some video.

In the video my husband showed me, our son walks several paces ahead, speeding away from his dad in an effort to prove he can do this on his own. Or maybe just to get away from the embarrassing parent with the embarrassing video camera.

My husband and I laughed about it together, but my throat grew tight.

So this is the way it's going to be, I thought.

This is the way it should be, I thought.

Our children are with us for only a small moment in time. They are fully dependent on us for food and safety and getting themselves places. And then they grow and become more competent on their own and want to do more independently, and we let them, necessarily, because it's a good learning experience. They still need us for so much. For enough.

And then comes the tearing away.

I see it in my oldest son, of course, but I also see it in my youngest, who is three and no longer wants to sit on my lap and snuggle and lay his head on my shoulder like he used to. My kisses have already lost their magic to heal his hurts.

There is a throbbing pain in this growing older, in this letting go, step by step by step. In this release from what seems to be the limiting confines of motherhood but which we see, once out of them, are really a beautiful responsibility.

Hindsight, you know. It has a lot to teach us.

On the first day of school, my son will navigate his classes with all the ease and anticipation with which he has navigated every stage of life; he does not need his dad and me for this. He will need us for other things, perhaps, but not this. He has left behind the walk to school, the walk to class, the kiss at the door, as he will leave behind other things in the coming years.

And I will grieve these leaving-behinds, of course, but I will also enjoy them. He is mine for only a small amount of time— and I will take what time I have and use it to its fullest.

Today I will brush his hair out of his eyes—the hair he must cut for athletics class—kiss the top of his forehead and ask him what he'd like to eat for breakfast. Instead of answering my question, he will tell me about a book he stayed up too late reading last night, and we will laugh, talk, connect for a moment or two, before going our separate ways in the house.

Love stretching long and elastic between us.

89. Growing Up is Never Easy

I could feel it coming: the nervous anticipation of the first day of school.

When I was a kid, I threw my nervous energy into choosing my first-day-of-school outfit (which got progressively more complicated as I grew older and cared more about first impressions). I would lay out my clothes, visualize the next morning, plan for the unexpected.

My sons are not so conscientious. I am the one who usually lays out their first-day-of-school outfit, not because they can't but because for now they humor me with a special coordinated outfit (which is not the same as matching, by the way; in their coordinated outfits I try to choose pieces that account for their color and style preferences and their personalities, within reason. No, the eight-year-old cannot wear a fluorescent orange Pokémon shirt the first day of school.) Once I've released the outfit, which I keep in my closet for security purposes until the night before the first day, they will stare at their shoes, drape socks over the sides, run their hands across their new backpacks, presumably thinking about what the next day will hold—or perhaps thinking nothing at all.

This year we had a brand-new experience for the first day of school: my oldest son was entering middle school. So the nervous energy that accompanies all first days of school held something else: a tinge of fear.

He hovered outside our bedroom, meandering in every so often so we could tell him, gently, that he needed to get to bed so he would be well rested for his first day. He lingered. He paged through books on my bedside table. He examined his fingernails.

I could tell he wasn't quite ready to close the door on summer. He knew—he knows—that life from here on out will be much different.

Growing up isn't always easy. I daily watch my sons pull against the tether that keeps them dependent on me, ever ready to assert their own independence, even if they're not quite capable yet. And then a new stage of life presents itself, and freedom widens, and they huddle at the precipice, peering over the edge, questioning whether they are actually ready. They wonder if they have what it takes to fly. They assess how hard the ground might be, because their safety net isn't quite as thick as it used to be (though this is just an illusion; they always have a thick safety net).

At some point, I drew my son nearer to me. I held his hand. I did not tell him he would be fine, school would be fun, everything would be easier than he thinks; none of that is assured. I only said, *Remember who you are.*

He knows what this means. Since our kids were young, any time we drop them off somewhere we will not be, we have told them, *Remember who you are: strong, kind, courageous, and mostly my son.* It's a phrase they have heard all their lives. It's a phrase that speaks of love—that they will always, no matter what, be loved.

An easy, fun, even good year is not assured my son; that's not how life works. But what *is* assured is that at the end of this next season of life, he will have grown, learned, and walked deeper into who he is. And no matter what kinds of twists and turns this year holds, no matter where he goes or what mistakes he makes or what victories he has, he will never be anything other than who he is: strong, kind, courageous, son.

Worthy.

Half an hour past his bedtime, he finally found his way back to his room, filled his diffuser with lavender essential oil, and read until he fell asleep, covers pulled up to his chin, book marked with a finger.

The same kid—but different.

90. We All Leave a Legacy

My husband burned popcorn tonight. I'm already in bed, but the smell of burned popcorn has a way of infiltrating everything. I imagine its shifting gray cloud, climbing up the stairs and into our room, hundreds of feet away from the kitchen. I wrinkle my nose.

He opened all the doors and windows downstairs so the night could steal inside (in the form of bugs and flies, which seem to be in abundance this time of year), adjusted all the vents, and turned on fans, hoping one of those efforts might usher out the pervasive smell. But it lingers.

Burning popcorn produces quite a lot of smoke, and moments ago, before I retreated to our room, my husband waved madly, trying to steer the smoke from the alarms so they wouldn't wake all the sleeping dragons in our house. He was successful at this. But the smell of burned popcorn remains, relentless but also, somehow, comforting.

We are like the smell of popcorn (the good kind, not the burned kind), lingering long after we've shriveled into dust.

91. Time Moves in Only One Direction

My youngest son, who just turned three, has been a little clingy lately, waking up with night terrors, begging to sleep with us. He follows me around the house like he doesn't want to let me out of his sight, like he's afraid to be alone. Something has frightened him—it's unclear what; he does not have the vocabulary to explain this fear. Not many young children do.

His clinging sometimes feels a bit suffocating.

For Christmas this year, he got some cute dinosaur slippers. He wears them everywhere—around the house, on the walk to his brothers' school, to the store. People comment on how adorable they are—and they're right.

The other day, he crashed into my room, where I was working. I said a quick hello and then I went back to work, fully engaged in writing whatever story I had open in front of me. And a few minutes later, I looked up to see him typing away at my grandmother's old Remington.

In his dinosaur slippers.

I watched, blinking away tears I couldn't explain. He's growing up, he'll soon get over his clinginess, he will not fit into these dinosaur slippers forever.

I made a note to myself: Don't miss the magnificent moments.

92. Smother Them in Love as Long as You Can

It happened while I wasn't looking: his legs lengthened, his jaw jutted, his eyebrows lost the pucker of flesh around them.

I blinked, and he turned twelve.

We've had a challenging year. This is my son's first year of middle school and keeping up with all the homework, the new dynamics with friends and teachers—sometimes he falters. Sometimes I falter.

It's been an uncharacteristically rainy season. The sky's grayness, the lack of light, the longer nights are all taking their toll on him. One minute he tells me something wise that he's been ruminating, the next minute he breaks down the lines of communication with a meltdown that shakes the walls.

I am always surprised by these displays. He has convinced me so thoroughly that he is all grown up, and then the whole world falls apart, reminds me that he is becoming a young man, but he is still a young boy. These things take time.

Growing up happens in jolts.

Yesterday afternoon my husband and I prepared dinner together in our kitchen. It's a rare occasion when both of us are available to cook and talk. My husband admitted that he felt like our son took advantage of my being gone the previous night (I'd attended a book club meeting with some friends); he'd barged into our room continuously, to tell his father something or other. I reminded my husband that our son needs him now more than ever—he was probably just looking for connection. We both moved out toward the library, where our long-legged son stretched out on the couch, his nose stuck in a book.

My husband grabbed my hand. He said, "He won't be here forever, will he?"

Neither one of us answered. It was a question that didn't need an answer.

Later that evening, when my son was on his way to spread some mustard on a sandwich, my husband caught him in his arms. My son leaned in like he always does—head first, no arms hugging back. He's getting too big for hugs, he thinks.

"All the way in," his father said.

My son laughed but obliged.

He moved toward the table, but I caught him, too. He said, "What do I have to do to make it to the table and put a little mustard on my sandwich?"

I wanted to say, "You will never, ever, ever be able to escape our love."

Instead, I laughed and let him go.

93. Let the Best Moments Banish Melancholy

How to banish melancholy
You will need:
A two-year-old boy
Evening time
A putting back to bed

It has become a ritual of sorts—this little boy gets out of bed while I am snuggling with his older brothers, and, rather than listening to my firm, "Please get back in your bed, sweet boy," he sits on the stairs and says, "No. Never." He says it with a half-smile, like we're playing a game, like he's hoping this night will be different from the last eleven.

I'm tired tonight. Melancholic. The melancholy hangs on many things, but mostly life—its pressures and disappointments. I have been writing a story about suicide, and it is unmooring me.

I don't want to go back in his room. All day I've been cleaning up after children, and all I really want to do is climb into bed, pull the covers up to my chin, and sleep.

But a sharp pain threads into my chest, and I remember: He is the last baby. And he is two. And he will not always be two. And this time—this precious, wonderful, exhausting, wonderful time—will not last forever.

So I go back into his room and kneel beside his toddler bed and snuggle with him for a few minutes. I tell him I love him so much. He tells me he loves me so much. I tell him he's growing up too fast. He tells me I'm growing up too fast. I laugh. He laughs.

And just like that, the melancholy is gone.

94. Squeeze the Joy out of Moments

Every Wednesday night, my oldest son and I have what we call "Snuggle Time." It's a sweet time—about fifteen minutes—when he gets to have my undivided attention—which is a precious rarity in our home.

The last two Snuggle Time sessions he's wanted to go for a walk—just up to our mailbox and back.

The other night, the moon shone nearly full. We stepped outside our house, and there it was to greet us, looming in the black sky, the stars around it hardly visible because of its luminance. For a moment, a cloud passed over it, turning it hazy, like a glowing orb, a little other-worldly.

"Look at the moon," my son said. We stood there for a few minutes, admiring this spectacle of the universe, which put on a lovely show, as though it knew we were watching. Then we continued on our mission: to the mailbox.

My son slipped his hand in mine, and we walked, side by side, step matched to step, the keys jangling in my other hand. He talked about what he wanted to do for his elective next year, when he enters middle school. I listened. I breathed. I saw.

Click. The stars peering out from behind clouds, pulsing a song we could not hear.

Click. The neighbors' cars, shadowed, shining after a thin blanket of rain earlier this evening.

Click. A cat stealing across the driveway.

We joked about what we would have done if the animal skittering across the driveway had not been a cat—a skunk, perhaps, or a raccoon or a zombie. (We would have run, of course.)

We were back at the house much too soon, so we stopped again, peered up at the moon, still as lovely as before, his hand still in mine. The insignificant mail shared space with the keys in my other hand. My gaze kept turning back to that brilliant moon, as if something waited for my notice. For my listening.

And I heard it: the earth sang.

The earth is always singing, I think. It may sound a bit mystical to say that, but I agree with John Keats: "The poetry of the earth is never dead."

And it has something to tell us if we take a moment to listen.

That night, it said, "Linger for a bit. Enjoy your son. Be here, now. Nothing lasts forever."

So I lingered. After the timer clanged, startling both of us in a way that made him laugh hysterically, I took an extra minute—two, three—with my son.

He will not always hold my hand. He will not always walk with me, to the mailbox and back. He will not always smile up at the moon.

Nothing lasts forever.

95. Seasons Come and Seasons Go

My head is spinning today. There are too many things on my mind, too many things to be done, too many words that need saying—and not enough spaces for them all. I feel burdened and anxious, but still I grasp at a positive attitude, because it's summer and I get to hang out with all my sons and I won't have that privilege much longer. So at the end of a rough day, here is where I land:

1. It won't always be this hard.
2. I won't always feel this overwhelmed.
3. A season only lasts so long, and then it's gone.

And I get back to work, saying what I can, doing what I can, thinking what I can in this season that will, in hindsight, fly like all the others.

96. Don't Fight Time, Move With It

Every time I look at him, he is a little bit older.

It's the way of things, the liquid movement of time, rippling toward a place where he is all the way grown, this first son of mine.

I worry about him. I worry about his heart, his mind, his fragile self-confidence. If he could see through my eyes, he would know that he is important, remarkable, so very loved. I worry that life will buffet him across the mountainous gaps and he will forget that he is important, remarkable, loved.

It is a mother's way to worry.

But there is also a golden joy that tinges the edges of this growing. To watch the young man he is becoming, to hear the passions and philosophies of his heart. To feel his presence, as large as a pre-teenager and yet larger even still, as he grows, steadily, into himself.

He begins middle school in the fall, yet another worry—and joy—to add to the list of them. The other night I told him, "Be prepared. I'm going to be really emotional at the end of this year and the summer and the beginning of your first year of middle school."

He smiled and nodded; he already knows. He already senses. It is not because of who he is or what he has done—it is because as he grows he takes another giant step away from me.

He knows it is love that makes me so emotional.

Last night we sat down to play Uno. He reveled in the massive number of good cards he had in his hand—already he had played several. I watched his smile, the way he examined his cards, the little gleam in his eyes that said he knew he was going to win. His face hides nothing.

And yet it hides everything—everything of his future, the man he will be, the things that await him.

At the end of our time together, I asked him for a hug and a kiss; he gave them to me—for now.

And another second passed, turning him older.

97. Carefully Balance Movement with Stillness

I'm entirely too busy most of the time.

I'm reading, I'm writing, I'm thinking about reading and writing, I'm strategizing, I'm cleaning up, I'm doing dishes, I'm responding to important messages.

But there is a boy, the one who came last in my lineup of sons, who will, at the most inopportune of times, come up to me and say, "Hi."

Sometimes I'm too distracted, my head buried in something or other, and I will just say a quick "hi" back and finish whatever I'm doing, at which point this little boy sticks his head on my book or pulls my phone out of my hands or steals my pen and tries again. "Hi," he says.

This always makes me laugh.

His words say more than "hi." They say, *I am here now. See me? Time goes fast, and I am your last.*

His words remind me to see, to take a step back into my world, to pay attention.

The problem is that there is always so much to do. My time is so short that I have to be regimented and rigid to make sure everything gets done—house runs smoothly, business stays afloat, dreams keep heading toward reality.

The other problem is that I also want to make sure I see all my sons, all the time. That I don't miss a thing. That I live fully present all the time.

It's not easy, balancing the two.

Often, I'll reflect on how days sometimes seem endless, when one of my sons is whining and another is stealing food, and then I'll watch them for a while and marvel at how much they've grown in so very little time. They are becoming young men, right before my eyes, and they will never stop. No one's ever found a way to reverse time.

And yet time's short supply demands I use it wisely, meaning I get things done.

I feel split by the dichotomy. Work or play? Sit still or move? Watch or check off more tasks?

It never feels like there's enough time. We race against time, try to save time, carve out time, capture a moment in time.

But there is time enough, if I use what I can to work and play and sit still and move and watch and check off more tasks.

My son's innocent game reminds me, today, to sit a little stiller, to watch, to capture.

Click. The sun stripes his face, his blue eyes glitter, his lips pucker out in concentration as he watches a fly zigging around his feet. I laugh as I say his name, breaking his concentration. He laughs, too.

Click. Another rests his face against the couch, his eyes staring at something I can't see, the blue of his shirt making his complexion look smooth and brown. One foot climbs over the other.

Click. The other one reclines on the arm of the couch, complaining a little, his hair parted away from his eyes. He smiles at something and blinks, long lashes fluttering. He is six today, gone tomorrow.

Times stretches between us as I look at all of them and

observe, fully immersed in my world.

Here's where it all begins, the living.

Later, when my youngest bends over a coloring book, concentrating hard on staying in the lines, I lean close, whisper, "Hi."

He looks up, grins, answers, "Hi."

Both of us seen, for another moment in time.

98. Time Pauses in the Moments

Today was my oldest son's birthday. He turned eleven.

I had no idea, eleven years ago, how wondrous the world could be, but a little boy would show me. I had no idea how paradoxical our lives could be—beautiful one moment and maddening the next—but a little boy would show me. I had no idea how excruciatingly painful and extraordinarily breathtaking love could be.

But a little boy would show me.

Motherhood has been a transformative journey of significant proportion; I've written at length about this transformation on other birthdays. My journey has been marked by self-discovery, self-sacrifice, and self-acceptance—but even more startling this year is this: It has also been marked by a gradual letting go. Inch by inch. Day by day.

My son is an adolescent now. He does not need me for as much as he used to. He will need me less next year than he needs me this one. When I think of this future that seems to speed so relentlessly forward, I want to slow time, rewind, go back all the way to the beginning.

Can we go back to the beginning?

No. Of course not.

If there is anything I have learned in the last month—dealing with a brain cancer diagnosis in someone I love, coming to terms with that uncertain future, wishing I could go all the way back to the beginning—it's this: The future can be a frightening, insecure, unassured possibility. The real living happens moment by moment by moment. Now.

So today I will not think about how my son will be driving in four years and graduating in seven and how he'll be grown and gone after that. I will see only the eleven-year-old boy—halfway in childhood, halfway out of it—dressed in a size large onesie, reading a Garfield comic strip collection in the most inconvenient spot on our floor (right in front of the stairs), and I will marvel at the gift his daddy and I have been given.

99. Taking Time In is Necessary to Well Being

If there is a lesson that summer teaches me more than anything else, it is this: In order to survive—and more than that: continue to exist in a place of joy and gratitude—I need time in.

When my sons were younger, my husband and I fell into a pretty regular practice of engaging them in what we called "time in." It was a regular practice because there were multiple opportunities for misbehavior due to immaturity and, mostly, threenager behavior.

It went like this: We would correct a behavior, our son would look at us in that overtly defiant way, and, without even trying to conceal his intention, he would repeat the behavior for which he'd just received correction. Correction escalated to time in—our son would sit on the couch beside us and we'd talk about the behavior, why it wasn't allowed, and let our son sulk about his removal from what he wanted to do. Once the proper amount of time had passed, he'd be free again to hopefully learn from his mistakes and amend his behavior.

We didn't enforce the typical time out, because we understood that misbehavior most often stems from a broken connection, and the best way to correct misbehavior was to reestablish connection, even if it was simply sitting on the couch beside the son who was temporarily removed from play.

In the years since those early days, I've continued to see the value of this practice, not just for my sons but for myself. In the daily routine and wear of life, particularly one filled with children and the needs they require, it takes hardly any time, at least for me, to feel burned out and restless, to reach a place where I'm longing for time in—time to watch them like an invisible observer or time to sit completely by myself, in solitude, and hear myself think.

I am never more aware of this than during the summer. One morning begins—I've just finished a run, kids are hungry, asking when breakfast will be on the table, someone didn't sleep well last night, the pineapple needs to be cut up, salad prepped for dinner, another load of laundry started, the back door's open, kettle is whistling, I don't know where I put the hot pad, my head is spinning, spinning, spinning.

Recently I confessed to my husband that sometimes I just feel like slipping into the car and driving away for a while. He nodded. I thought maybe he didn't understand fully what I was saying, so I amended: "Not a while, meaning hours," I said. "A while meaning days. Weeks, maybe."

"Why don't you?" he said.

I laughed. Why don't I? Because things would fall apart. I'm needed here. Moms don't get breaks, at least not extended ones.

For a while, I've been longing to go away on a self-imposed writing retreat—all by myself, to some place beautiful. But there's always a reason not to—financial constraints, time, I'm needed here.

Guilt. Yes, that's the big one.

But the truth is, just like my sons once needed the "time in" to re-center and find their peace and joy and courage and compassion again, so do we all. Sometimes life gets to be too much—too much disappointment, too much responsibility, too much pressure, too much activity—and it's necessary to take a step back, to say, My heart, my well being, my sanity (because sometimes it's simply that) needs this time in—this space where nothing is expected of me, where I am my own person, where my petals can begin to unfold and soak up the sunshine again.

And when guilt starts gathering on our shoulders, as it so often does (especially for women), it's worthwhile to remember: What we are showing our children, our spouses, the people around us in our spheres of influence, is that we are important enough to prioritize—which means they, too, are important enough to prioritize.

I often wonder how the world might be different if, in moments of overwhelm, anger, disappointment, grief, hurt, fear, we took a moment or two—days, maybe—for a time in.

Love collected so it can then be shared.

100. Remember: Time Is Its Own Master

My driver's license was four months expired.

I didn't notice this earlier, because I don't usually drive anywhere. When I get out of the house, I either walk, run, or let my husband drive me. I don't have much need for a driver's license anymore, except when I do.

Today I needed to vote, and I walked into the room set aside at my sons' elementary school. Two elderly men sat manning the polls. They recalled that they had seen my husband vote today; they remembered the street name, "Fire Cracker" for the explosive picture it brought to mind. When they asked for my photo identification, I told them that it was expired, that I hadn't yet had a chance to renew it, that I didn't actually know it was expired until I took it out of my wallet this morning. Maybe that wasn't entirely true. Maybe I knew its expiration intuitively; I seem to remember thinking about it, briefly, on my birthday this year, because I didn't want to visit the DMV, which always feels like a time sink. But I never confirmed whether or not it needed renewal, and the days passed and the months after, too.

The tallest of the two men took the license from me and said that as long as it wasn't four years expired, I would be able to use it. Four years expired! How does anyone let their license lapse into four years' expiration? I thought about how the month of my birthday turned into four months later, and I figured it would be quite easy, actually, for four months to turn into four years. Time speeds by. I am forever trying to still it, but it never listens.

The men laughed about my canned joke, which I use everywhere I'm able: My husband and I live on Fire Cracker, and we are the parents of six boys, which makes our street name situationally appropriate: Our house is, itself, a firecracker.

Then I vote, and the men wave me out. "Enjoy those boys," one of them calls just before I'm out the door.

In his words were the four months that turn into four years, the sleek and slippery nature of time. I smiled. "Thank you. I will," I returned. I put my expired license in my pocket and headed back home to my hungry sons, waiting for a dinner I enjoyed cooking for once, if only for the reminder that time speeds and never ever slows.

Visit www.racheltoalson.com for more of Rachel's books.

About the Author

Rachel has been practicing the fine art of essay writing for more than a decade. She is the kind of reader who enjoys reading the thoughts and philosophies of others, however they may differ from her own, because she believes that we all have significant contributions to make in the lives of others.

When she is not buried in the pages of a new essay collection, Rachel enjoys writing poetry and fiction for adults, young adults, and kids. She is the author of *The Colors of the Rain*, a middle grade novel-in-verse; *The Woods*, a middle grade fantasy realism novel; six humor essay books, one (completely serious) essay book, six poetry books, and seventeen middle grade fantasy books under a pen name.

She lives with her husband of seventeen years and her six sons in San Antonio, Texas.

www.racheltoalson.com

A Note from Rachel

My dear reader,

I sincerely hope you have enjoyed these short meditations on a variety of topics (though, in reading and editing this manuscript, it's clear I spend an inordinate amount of time thinking about and dwelling on time). I hope that, in some way, they have both enlightened and encouraged you to live your best life, to bravely face your challenges, and to radically love even the most difficult-to-love people. It is a privilege and an honor to be even just a small tiny piece of repairing the world—one person's world—and cheering my fellow humans on in their world-changing endeavors.

Please don't hesitate to send me a note and connect (rachel@racheltoalson.com), and if you feel so inclined, leave a review of this book (reviews help increase a book's visibility so it can get into the hands of more readers) and pass it along to the people in your life who need it the most.

Thank you for reading my humble thoughts. May you be brave, strong, and kind all the days of your life.

In love,
Rachel

Acknowledgments

This book would not have made it past the pages of my journal without:

Ben—Thanks for working so hard on the graphics, sending out my newsletters, and for always being such a relentless advocate for (and believer in) me and my career.

Asa and Hosea—Thanks for babysitting your brothers so Daddy and I can have our grocery store date.

Jadon—Thanks for being you—epic arguments, food thievery, and all.

Boaz and Zadok—Thanks for showing me what patience means and also the limitless nature of love.

Asher—Thanks for your well timed hugs.

(Do you all know how very loved you are by this lucky woman?)

My sons' schools—Thanks for giving me an option besides homeschooling, because…well, I'm no good at it. And thanks for providing me with SO MANY HOURS to get work done!

Memama, Nana, Memaw, Mom, Aunt Lynette—all the wise women in in my life—thanks for being your wondrous selves.

God—Thanks for showing yourself in unexpected, miraculous ways.

Reader Library

Speak to Me of Life is a collection of short essays on love, children, identity, anxiety, and creativity, among many other topics. But mostly it is a book about life—life lived to its fullest. Life lived in love, freedom, and joy. Life lived without fear.

Rachel takes her readers on a trip through the inner terrain of a heart, stopping only to say, in conclusion: Don't be afraid to be you.

Get *Speak to Me of Life* FREE for a limited time:

Visit* racheltoalson.com/freebook

*Must be 13 or older to be eligible

Enjoy more titles from Rachel Toalson

racheltoalson.com

www.ingramcontent.com/pod-product-compliance
Lightning Source LLC
Chambersburg PA
CBHW030321100526
44592CB00010B/517